UGLY
TRUTH
about
SMALL
BUSINESS

Never-Saw-It-Coming
50 THINGS THAT CAN GO WRONG...
and What You Can Do About It

Ruth King

SOURCEBOOKS, INC.®
NAPERVILLE, ILLINOIS

Copyright © 2005 by Ruth King
Cover and internal design © 2005 by Sourcebooks, Inc.
Sourcebooks and the colophon are registered trademarks of Sourcebooks, Inc.

This publication is designed to provide accurate and authoritative information in regard to the subject matter covered. It is sold with the understanding that the publisher is not engaged in rendering legal, accounting, or other professional service. If legal advice or other expert assistance is required, the services of a competent professional person should be sought.—*From a Declaration of Principles Jointly Adopted by a Committee of the American Bar Association and a Committee of Publishers and Associations*

All brand names and product names used in this book are trademarks, registered trademarks, or trade names of their respective holders. Sourcebooks, Inc., is not associated with any product or vendor in this book.

Published by Sourcebooks, Inc.
P.O. Box 4410, Naperville, Illinois 60567–4410
(630) 961-3900
FAX: (630) 961-2168
www.sourcebooks.com

ISBN 13: 978-1-4022-0514-9

Library of Congress Cataloging-in-Publication Data

King, Ruth.
  The ugly truth about small business: 50 things that can go wrong and what you can do about it / Ruth King.
     p. cm.
  Includes index.
  1-4022-0514-7 (alk. paper)
  1. Small business—Management—Handbooks, manuals, etc. I. Title.

HD62.7.K567 2005
658.02'2—dc22

                                        2005017686

Printed and bound in the United States of America.
VP 10 9 8 7 6 5 4 3

This book is dedicated to the millions
of small business owners who
are thinking about starting,
have started,
or are operating their own small businesses.
I hope the stories you read on the following pages
give you comfort, hope, ideas, and
the knowledge that you are not alone.

To David,
Enjoy and pump
from this book.

CONTENTS

<u>Part One</u>: 50 Stories of the Ugly Truth about Small Business

<u>Part Two</u>: What You Can Do about It

Chapter 3: 15 Critical Survival Strategies 247

Chapter 4: Realities of Partners 267

FOREWORD

YOU ARE NOT ALONE

My grandfather always said there are three types of businesspeople.

The first type makes mistakes and doesn't learn from them. These people make the same mistakes again.

The second type of businessperson makes mistakes and learns from them. They don't make those mistakes again.

The third type of businessperson learns from the mistakes of others so they never make those mistakes themselves. Of course, they do make some. But by learning from the mistakes of others, they save themselves time, headaches, and money. *The Ugly Truth about Small Business: 50 Things That Can Go Wrong and What You Can Do about It* will help you be the third type of businessperson.

Let's face it. As small business owners when we're asked, "How's business?" we respond, "Great!" even if our largest customer went bankrupt, we have three cents in the bank, and we don't know where the money for payroll is going to come from. We rarely trust anyone with the real story of how we're doing.

I started my first business in 1979. I was twenty-two years old. At that time, I didn't really appreciate how difficult and rewarding owning a business could be. After all, I still had the idealistic thought that starting and running a business was easy. Idealism turned to realism, struggle, and success. By the time I had my business for a few years, I wasn't sure whether being an entrepreneur was a blessing or a curse. I did know that I wanted control over my own destiny and owning a business was the best way to do it for me.

Over the past twenty-five years, I have been involved with seven businesses. Four of the seven were successful, two are too new to know whether they will be successful, and the seventh crashed as badly as you can crash.

It was at that time I took a job to generate some cash. Initially, it was great. The stress was off. I didn't have to worry about payroll and I had a steady paycheck. Within six months, I hated it. When I left eighteen months later, I swore that I would never work for anyone else again. Somehow, I would find a way to survive on my own. It took my husband and me several years to climb out of that $700,000 hole.

Each time I built a new business, the challenges became harder and harder. They were getting more complex. The simple business was a T-shirt company whose target market was student chapters of professional engineering societies. Our goal was to generate enough profit to go to the mountains each year and design the new T-shirts. We succeeded.

The complex business is one of the latest, the start-up of ProNetworkTV, Inc., television on the Internet for vertical markets. This start-up gave me the worst nightmare I've ever experienced: the loss of a $1.6 million contract, $800,000 in investment, and a "partner" the same day.

After this experience, I became fascinated with the risk aspects of business from a human, rather than a statistical, standpoint. I began to wonder why I continued. Why does anyone put themselves through the stress, the sleepless nights, and the fear? What was it in us that made us keep going?

I found out that I wasn't alone. I realized that each of the 23 million small business owners in the United States has their own personal challenges and triumphs owning a small business. Many don't have a place to turn when things aren't going well. After all, we entrepreneurs can be a tight-lipped bunch. *The Ugly Truth about Small Business: 50 Things That Can Go Wrong and What to Do about It* is the place to turn.

This book includes the stories of fifty entrepreneurs who graciously agreed to share their business stories. You'll find sole proprietorships, partnerships, and corporations; start-up businesses to multi-million dollar corporations; service businesses, manufacturing businesses, and everything in between. You'll read about some businesses that made it and so didn't.

When you read their stories, you will find that each defined their entrepreneurial nightmares personally. You might not think his or her experience was "so bad." However, it was terrifying for that person to go through it. Some stayed in their businesses; others closed their businesses and started another one. Still others closed their business and found other ways to support themselves and their families. Others are living the nightmares right now. They don't know whether the light at the end of the tunnel is a train headlight or real daylight.

All were generous to share their experiences with those of you who are running your businesses or thinking about starting a business. Some asked that I change their names and industries. I honored their requests. Their stories are accurate even though the names are not. Everyone shared with me so that you could learn from his or her experiences and avoid some stress.

This is a book of inspiration...of hope...and the comfort of knowing that you are not alone. When you read these stories and the ideas other business owners have used to solve their crises, you'll gain the knowledge that you can—and will—get through the challenges you face as a business owner. You'll learn from the experiences of others and become the third type of business owner.

INTRODUCTION

LEARNING FROM OUR MISTAKES

Whether you are thinking about starting a business, are in the midst of running a business, or have discontinued a business, you are not alone. There are millions of experienced, current, and former business owners who can supply perspective, inspiration, and guidance. All you have to do is ask.

I know. Most business owners keep to themselves. We've trusted people with our problems and gotten hurt. As a result, we don't trust ourselves to talk about the reality of where we are...except perhaps to a few individuals who probably have never started or run a business. Perhaps that's our greatest weakness as business owners. We rarely share and we don't ask for help. After all, we know that we're right and will go through the hard times to prove it.

People *are* willing to share. All you have to do is ask. I found this out when I was researching this book. So where do you find someone you can trust?

Sometimes it is a stranger. You've read an article by a person who sounds like you. You send that person an email. Surprise—you get a response, and that person is willing to help.

You can start a conversation on an airplane with the person sitting next to you. On planes, you can get into deep discussions because there is no fear; it's unlikely that you'll ever see that person again. People share a lot on airplanes. I know, I've traveled over two million miles and have talked to thousands of people on airplanes.

You can get the courage to call, write, or email a person who you admire. It's in a non-competitive business and that person has achieved success in your eyes. Offer to buy that person's breakfast, lunch, or dinner. You'll be amazed at what you can learn for the cost of a meal. It works. How do you get their attention? The best way that I've found is to send an overnight letter. Then you must have a reason that person should spend his or her valuable time with you. Be honest—sometimes the reason is just to pick that person's brain. After all, they've been through what you are going through. Finally, you have to be flexible and adjust your schedule to fit into that person's available time. Go to the meeting prepared with a list of questions (don't be surprised if the person wants you to submit the questions in advance). Take notes and learn from that person's wisdom.

The Ugly Truth about Small Business: 50 Things That Can Go Wrong and What You Can Do about It will give you ideas for getting through the tough nights, the lack of cash flow, and the many other things that are a reality when you run a business.

When you get to the other side and have a successful or unsuccessful business, be willing to share your experiences with the next person who is about to embark on or is living the American dream of owning his own business. He or she will have sleepless nights, stress, fear, and survival challenges. Offer a helping hand to get him or her through.

CHAPTER ONE

WHY WE ARE ENTREPRENEURS

In a word, passion. We have passion for what we do. There are many other reasons after passion, but the overriding factor is that we love what we do. Education level doesn't matter. Funding doesn't matter. We are - entrepreneurs because we see a need, enjoy doing something, or want to do something and the only way to get it done is through a business of our own.

Jeff Benjamin, CEO of Breakthrough Training, put it very succinctly. "I think one of the biggest things for me that has always kept me going is that I am so passionate about what I do, so failing or not making it or not being successful is just not an option."

Following are more reasons why we are entrepreneurs.

Entrepreneurs and Corporate America Don't Fit

We don't fit the corporate world. So many of the entrepreneurs told me that they made the leap because they were tired of not being recognized for their accomplishments. By starting their businesses, they eventually were recognized for their efforts. Others started in the corporate world and found it lacking. Some started in the corporate world and the corporate world found them lacking.

Sally Veillette brought her former company the largest sale they ever made, over four million dollars. She built a division. Then, she quit. When asked why, she said, "Once you decide to let yourself explore and learn what you really love to do with the people you love to do it with, you can't stop. It takes on a vitality of its own. You've made the decision to do it and you don't want to stop the flow. It is the driving factor that gives you the energy to continue to go through the dark spots and go on with your dream."

> *We became entrepreneurs because we have a passion for what we are doing.*

Kathy Bedell Mayo's comment sums up many of the reasons why people leave the "comfort and security" of a corporate job: "I was tired of the corporate America rat race. I felt that I was being held in bondage: working hard for minuscule raises that fell within the bell curve of acceptability. I decided to do what I love doing and I quit."

Most entrepreneurs don't fit the corporate mold. We chafe at the restrictions and don't like following rules (unless we make them). Eventually, we get frustrated and start our own businesses to have control over our own destiny.

We Have No Other Choice

Sometimes we don't see it coming. A reluctant and surprised entrepreneur was told that he should have his own business because he didn't fit into the corporate mold. He was forced into the opportunity when he was fired from his job.

Pauline Cormier needed to find a project because her husband was on strike. That propelled her to start her business.

Some people found their way to entrepreneurship after making the comments to their bosses that they wanted to be in business for themselves. This is the case for Doug Kruse, who told his boss that he wanted to have his own business. Doug actually made it easy for his boss to decide whom to lay off when layoffs were necessary. Doug got his wish.

Another reason entrepreneurs have is to establish credit. This was the case with Kitty Ariza. She was married, but all of the credit was in her husband's name. She wanted her own credit. It took several years and dealing with new businesses who were willing to take a risk on her, but she got it.

Others got the opportunity by accident. One of the entrepreneurs was told that if he didn't do a business by the time he was thirty-five, he wouldn't get the opportunity to be successful. He was thirty-four and a situation arose where he had an opportunity to be on his own. With the support of his wife, he jumped into business.

It's in Our Blood

We've always known we would have our own business and are willing to take the risks. Some, like Christine Kloser, knew it from the time they were young and never tried to fit in. She always knew that she was different from her high school classmates who were set on going to college and getting a job. She knew that wasn't for her.

Still others have known from the time they were children that they would be in business. Even though I had my first "real business" at twenty-two, I started selling things in my childhood. Many had paper routes. Many invested in stock markets. Most had made money as a child.

Many, many failed in their first attempts. Bob Breaux knew he was destined to have his own business. When the first one failed, he got a job to tide him over until he got the next opportunity. Others went searching from one business to another. All learned from their mistakes, continued on, and eventually had a successful business.

Despite all of the trials and tribulations, every - entrepreneur who had been in the corporate world before starting or buying their business, says that being in business is better than being in the corporate world.

For those who have built multimillion dollar businesses, they've remembered what it was like for them and tried to create a better business environment.

Entrepreneurs become entrepreneurs because we have a passion for what we are doing. Sometimes, we are forced into business. Sometimes, we make a conscious decision to be in business. We put up with the stress, the fear, and the hard times because we are trying to make a difference in the world, each in our own way.

CHAPTER TWO

MY STORY

Ruth King
CEO, ProNetworkTV, Inc. and BusinessTVChannel.com

I had been working on a large broadcast-training project with a customer for nearly a year. It was going well, moving right along. We had a letter from the customer that was better than a letter of intent. They were already paying us for a small project. The letter was used to secure funding from investors. The additional funds would be invested when the formal contract was signed.

We were ready to begin the real work when the telephone rang. The customer said, "The budget has been cut and the $1.6 million expenditure for the project is a casualty." In that instant, the company and I both came crashing down. I had put $500,000 in the company over the last year, and in my mind, it was gone. And I had a "partner" who wouldn't put money into the business. I was stunned.

I walked out of the building and found a spot where I could be by myself. I cried until there were no more tears. I kept hearing my father's voice: "When bad things happen, you pick yourself up, dust yourself off, and keep going." This was time to get on with it. But what to do with all of the people, the payroll, and the debt load? Did I have enough guts to make the tough decisions that had to be made? I was sure I did not. I couldn't. I was numb.

> *Pick yourself up, dust yourself off, and keep going.*

Thanksgiving Day 2001 was the worst Thanksgiving of my life. I spent it in tears. Thankful? What did I have to be thankful for? The world I had so carefully and lovingly crafted crashed, and it landed right on me.

Nothing was right. I was frustrated. I was hurt. I thought that I could rely on my partner. I couldn't. Worst of all, I stopped believing in myself.

My husband came to my rescue. Despite all of the negativity around me, he kept telling me that I had to get the company up. I had to start broadcasting. I didn't hear him at first. He got louder and finally we had a huge fight about it. I finally heard him. He believed in me more than I did.

So, over the objections of my partner and more than a few employees, I used the last of the credit on my credit cards and started building the world's least expensive studio for broadcasting on the Internet. During the three months of building, I had arguments with the employees. They objected to what I wanted to do. I fired some, laid off others, and then all but a few were gone. My partner fought hardest against building the small studio. That should have been a warning sign.

Thinking about it later, I realized that since Christmas, my partner's focus was on finding a job and getting paid until he found one, rather than helping us get started and generate revenues. He had no fat in the fire and, therefore, no risk. I had taken all the risk, put in all the money, as well as heart and soul. Soon, he too was gone.

On March 13, 2002, with the help of my husband, his partner, and a few loyal employees who stuck with us, we began broadcasting out of our new small, 15 x 25-foot studio. There were thirteen viewers.

Now there are over three thousand. Everyone who said that we couldn't do it after the loss of the contract was proven wrong. We did it and continue to broadcast today.

The model was so successful that we started broadcasting to our next target market: Entrepreneurs like us. BusinessTVChannel.com began airing programs on January 3, 2005.

What I learned:

A partner isn't a partner if you're the only one investing dollars in the business. He is an employee and will not have the same interests as you do, no matter what he says.

My father was right. You can pick yourself up, dust yourself off, and keep going. Sometimes you just need someone who can provide a boost up. Find that person.

Applying the lessons learned to your business:

If you are going into business with a partner, make sure that you ask a series of very critical questions before you begin:

- What money are you committing to the business?
- What happens if the company needs money?
- Will you "sign on the dotted line" personally?

This will show you the commitment of the partner. If the partner won't commit personal assets and you are committing assets, then you don't have a partnership. You are the boss and your so-called partner is an employee.

Make sure that you have people outside the business whom you can count on for ideas, talk with, and from whom you can get ideas. They can help you through the dark days.

Instead of relying on one big customer, we decided to find many smaller customers. You can start with a small number. We had only thirteen when we began broadcasting. The critical thing is to prove that people will use your products. Once you find that first customer, others will follow.

PART ONE

50 STORIES OF THE UGLY TRUTH ABOUT SMALL BUSINESS

#1

I BOUGHT THE WRONG BUSINESS
Bob Breaux

CEO, Total Computer Systems, Inc.

I was destined to have my own business. I guess that, deep down, people have a sense of creativity. You can mold it, fix it, and do it. I bought a printing company in 1979. The former owner had several locations in a business that required on-site owner management. He was trying to operate them as a remote owner. I mortgaged my house for thirty thousand dollars more than it was worth and bought 80 percent of the company.

I couldn't operate all of the locations either. The company folded in two years. It should have folded in six months. Ah, the perpetual optimist.

When I left, I gave the business back to the previous owner. He filed bankruptcy. I had nothing and couldn't make anything of it. It was very terrifying. I had no job, no money. We had a mortgage on the house for more than it was worth, plus car notes and other debt. We thought we'd be on the street in a matter of weeks.

I also made the mistake of not insisting that my name be taken off the corporate records. I would go out for my early morning run, and when I got back, the sheriff was waiting to serve me legal papers. That was an extremely intense, scary time. It turned out to be a big turning point in our lives. It did bring the family closer together and made us realize what was important. Our friends were phenomenally supportive. We have a tremendous faith in God and are very churchgoing. Our faith and our friends just came through for us.

My wife said that she never wanted to go through this again. She didn't care what kind of money I made. She wanted the security. I sat her down and told her she was going to have to get over that because I had to do it again. Finally, she said okay.

Maybe deep down it was to prove I could do it or that I wasn't a failure. I just knew that my lot in life was to operate a business and be my own boss.

We weren't put out on the street. I ended up getting a job and working until I got enough money to go back into business. Two years later, in 1983, I came across another opportunity to start my own business. I met someone who wanted me to go into the computer buying business with him.

I never gave up, even when I failed.

After looking at his business plan and watching his operation, I realized that he had blown all of his investment dollars. I wasn't going to make that mistake again.

By accident, I met the attorney that had helped me get out of the printing business. He asked me what I was doing. I told him I had thought about going into this business, but had decided to sidestep it. He said, "Well, why don't you do it on your own?" I told him, "You darn well know that I don't have any money." He replied,

"I do, so let's go." The problem was that the attorney wanted controlling interest.

I went to my CPA and asked him what he thought. He surprised me and said that he wanted to be in this with me. His partner also wanted in. I started Total Computer Systems, Inc. I am still in this business today.

I never gave up, even when I failed.

What I learned:

- Although I was terrified at the time, I kept going and kept the faith.
- Your spouse and friends can give great emotional support.
- You never know when the next business or business idea will appear. Many times, it is by a chance meeting.

Applying the lessons learned to your business:

Make a list of a hundred or more people you know who you think are successful. In your opinion, they may be successful financially, spiritually, raising children, or in other ways. The list should have their names, telephone numbers, and email addresses (if known). Meet with one of the people on the list each week. Find out how they became successful. What hardships did they go through? You might find yourself opening up to that person about your current situation. You'll definitely feel better. This should help you keep the faith. As a bonus, during some of the meetings you'll get ideas that will help you survive and start or grow your business.

This story has a "P.S.":

The ownership structure of Total Computer Systems, Inc., changed over the years. Originally, each of us owned 33 percent. During the course of running the business, my CPA partner got out. I put more money in by refinancing my house again. I wanted to make it an 80/20 stock split. My CPA agreed. He said to make out two stock certificates; each for 10 percent of the stock. When I handed him the certificates, he turned them over, assigned one to each of my two children, and handed them back to me! I broke down crying.

Years later I still break down telling this story. He has remained my CPA and has proudly watched the business grow over the years. As bad as it was the first time, I have smart, generous people watching my back this time.

#2

BATTLE SCARS
Tim Hutchinson

I could have been the biggest mass murderer the United States has ever known. As a child I was physically and verbally abused, and thought that love happened only on television. I slept in the corner of the basement; at night, my dad would come down and beat me for reasons unknown to me. By the time I was twelve years old, I was a cold, heartless child who began carrying a gun to school.

One day I decided I'd had enough of the torture and was going to check out of this earth. I was determined to not go alone. I felt compelled to take others with me. I felt harassed at home and I felt harassed at school. As much as I despised my parents, I simply couldn't kill my family. So, I made up my mind to kill as many people in my school as possible. I happened to know someone who was selling stolen military weapons, and was able to obtain lots of ammunition, some explosives, and a machine gun guaranteed to work. Fortunately, I was stopped a block and a half from school; less than five minutes away from killing over four hundred people.

A plan will keep you pointed straight at your goals.

Eventually my life was turned around because of a Holocaust survivor, who taught me important lessons and the value of life in America. I am now married with kids and reach out to lost and hurting teens every chance I get. I knew that if I could get my story out, I could help many more teens by showing them how to escape from the tangled web of pain and violence that a lot of them feel trapped in. So, that is what I did. I started a business to tell my story through books and talks at high schools.

I didn't know how difficult that would be. I should have put a big sign on my wall, "WARNING: You Have Entered Shark Infested Waters!" Despite my street smarts, I trusted people I knew better than to trust. I searched the Internet for information on publishing. I thought I could trust what I read. I didn't know the publishing business well, and proved to be an easy target. I lost tens of thousands of dollars on so-called experts. Yet I knew I had a story that had to be told and passed on. I discovered I needed a business plan, solid advice, and a game plan.

Things got so bad that I sold my new truck to pay for expenses. I found some associations, went to their meetings, read their materials, and joined them after seeing their results. I finally got the book published, then discovered that distribution was the key. Realizing I had to get the attention of the largest bookstores in the United States, I tried the standard route of contacting them via phone and email. The results were less than joyful. In fact, they were dismal. Then I had an idea: do a Google search on the companies' financial records and see if I could find a contact for a corporate executive. Then, I would ask (beg) that person for help. After an hour of browsing, I saw an email address for none other than the chief financial officer (CFO) of one of the biggest booksellers.

I knew emailing him was a real long shot, but figured I had nothing to lose, and everything to gain. I composed a one-paragraph email explaining my situation and asked for his help.

I remember clicking the "send" button and thinking my email would likely either be deleted as spam before being read, or intercepted by an executive assistant who would then delete it. Nonetheless, I hoped for the best.

I got a reply only thirty minutes later—and it was from the CFO himself! I was thrilled to learn that he would ensure the changes needed would be taken care of by the end of the week. My long shot had paid off. Hooray for entrepreneurial creativity! Three cheers for taking a chance!

My business was finally underway. Today it is thriving, my story is being told, and I'm helping many, many kids. In fact, I have great satisfaction knowing that already I have prevented two Columbine-type incidents! And I've only just begun.

What I learned:

- There is a lot of information on the Internet—some credible, mostly not. Don't believe everything that you read online. Be sure to check credentials, ask for references, and check them out. (Reading testimonials on a website doesn't count!)
- You have to have a plan from start to finish. It doesn't mean that it will happen exactly that way, but you won't go zigzagging either. I found out that a plan is like a living, breathing document and though it should change as situations dictate, it should also keep you pointed straight at your goals.

- Join a large association. Four of the five people I consider very trustworthy in business I found through an association. Ask questions—but be careful whose advice you take.
- Believe in yourself and your message.

Applying the lessons learned to your business:

- There are many places to go for help creating a business plan. Hundreds of books have been written about this subject. Government agencies such as the Service Corps of Retired Executives (SCORE) and the Small Business Administration (SBA) can also supply formats for the plan. If you are searching for a loan, then ask your banker for his preferred format for a business plan. If you are applying for a Small Business Administration loan, you have to follow the format supplied by the SBA.
- Your business plan is your road map. It defines your goals and outlines the steps you will take to reach them.
- Join associations dedicated to your type of business. These groups can help you create a practical plan. Find out what their members did to become successful. Learn from their mistakes.

#3

THE GRAVE DANCER
Ron Detjen
President and CEO, ImproMed, Inc.

I've always been a grave dancer. I couldn't afford anything when I started in business. I had to buy something that had problems—a business or a building that needed turning around—so I could afford it. I always had to modify it and do a lot to make it successful. I had some good fortune doing this and some good experiences. I had built profitable, successful businesses over the years using the bank's money. But my banker almost put that to an end in an afternoon. Here's my story.

I was trained in electronics in the Navy. When I was discharged, I couldn't do specific electronic work. I looked for a job in Wisconsin that I could make some money at. I started working as an ironworker because I never had a fear of heights and it paid a lot of money. I forgot how cold it was in Wisconsin. That wasn't going to last.

I went to Mexico with a friend, $125, and my first business venture. It blew up. I came out of Mexico starving. When I say starving, I am serious. I was in bad shape. We didn't have any money and we came home with literally three cents in our pockets.

Eventually, I found I was very good at selling. I was asked to teach sales. But I got bored with it. I had to go into business for myself.

I loved foreign cars. It was a time when everyone thought foreign cars might become 2 or 3 percent of the total cars in the U.S. I was convinced that they were going to be 20 percent, so I opened up a gas station in Oshkosh, Wisconsin, that specialized in repairing foreign cars. It expanded into a body shop, which expanded to a parts store, and then on into Green Bay, Wisconsin.

Not totally satisfied with owning only a gas station, body shop, and more, I was buying distressed duplexes and fixing them up. Then I began to convert duplexes to commercial properties. One of the commercial properties I owned had a tenant that was a veterinarian. He was building a computer system and I had some background in the computer industry from my time in the Navy.

The veterinarian was a good guy who got in trouble. He had an opportunity to sell the company, so he did. When he sold it, he got no cash; only shares of a publicly traded company that soon tanked.

I had a pretty good reputation in the community at that time as being a hardcore capitalist entrepreneur. He asked if there was any way I could put a group together to salvage this. My answer, of course, was yes. We negotiated a deal, and the next thing I knew, I was running this veterinarian software business along with my real estate, car washes, and other ventures I was involved in.

All of the businesses' accounts, loans, and real estate, including my own home, were with one bank that I had a great relationship with.

Back in those days, you generally established a relationship with a local bank. They looked at you and they looked at your financials and your accomplishments. I had accomplished a lot by then. Everything was running smoothly and I was current on everything, with nothing bouncing or any past due accounts. Then, a new president took over and almost killed everything.

I owed the bank about $3 million. The line of credit for the veterinarian software company was an unsecured line of credit for $500,000. One day I got a call from my loan officer. He said that the president of the bank wanted to talk with me. I had to be there at one o'clock the next day, and bring one of my business partners. It was a little odd that the president wasn't coming to see me, but I didn't think anything of it.

Fear ends when you think logically to solve problems.

My partner and I went to the bank and sat waiting for the president to show up. 1:00 came. 1:15 came. 1:30 came. Finally, at about 1:45, in walked the president of the bank, with an attorney I know. The attorney said "hi" to me, but the president of the bank never even spoke to me.

I was concerned because usually the bankers come to me, and I'm not asked to come to the bank. I wasn't told what this was about and then he didn't show up on time. We walked over to the president's office. I said, "Hi, you wanted to see me today. What do you want?"

These were his exact words. "I want you to get all your f—ing accounts out of this bank today." Terror hit. I said, "What are you talking about?" He said, "I don't want your f—ing loans in here, I don't want your personal stuff in here and you have some sort of stupid PECFA loan in here that is almost $250,000 that we pay the interest and that's not legal."

I said, "Not correct." He countered, "Yes it is and I don't want to hear anything more about it."

The bank president was screaming. Everyone in the office could hear him. I was in shock. He wanted my checking account and everything out that day. He said if I didn't, they would start actions against every one of my items. I told him I had payroll to make that Friday (the meeting was on a Tuesday). He said he really didn't care. He told me I was not using the line of credit to do it. The avalanche was about ready to begin.

I walked out of there reeling. My partner was in tears. I was very angry. I went back to work thinking, "Oh boy, all these years of work and this whole thing is going to roll on back down. It's going to be a matter of selling assets and seeing if I can keep everything together." I just stayed at work and thought about it.

I finally went home. It was the only time, in all of the years, my wife had ever seen me worried and stressed out about what I was going to do. I just didn't see any way out. My world was crashing in because of an irrational bank president who didn't know what he was doing when it came to loans.

Once the emotion stopped, I started thinking rationally. I just took one thing at a time. I called my trusted attorney. I knew that the most critical thing was payroll. Together we went over all of the loan agreements and developed a plan. By Friday, I had called my loan officer. I told him I wanted to talk to the president of the bank. He said no, I couldn't do that. So I said, "He needs to talk to my attorney then. The bank will honor my line of credit to pay payroll because of the agreement the bank signed with me. I will be running a payroll and those checks will clear."

I got a message from the president by phone saying the bank will honor the line of credit until the end of the month.

With that critical loan time bomb off my back, I then had the time to tackle each of the loan agreements individually. My reputation was known in the community, so it took me less than thirty days to find other banks to assume the loans. All of the loans were out of the original bank within sixty days.

What I learned:

- I don't keep all my business at one bank anymore.
- Business actions didn't bother me until this one. It was the only time I've ever let emotion take over rationality. Fear begins when emotions take over logic. Fear ends when you think logically to solve problems.

Applying the lessons learned to your business:

- Cultivate relationships with several banks and sources of funding. You might get your first loan from one bank. However, your personal banking might be with a different bank. Or, have several personal and business accounts. This way, if relationships sour with one bank, you have history built up with several banks.
- If you have built a relationship with one banker and he leaves that bank, follow him to his new bank. The bank your banker left will introduce you to another person at that bank. Your current bank wants to keep your business and will assign another person to your accounts. Get to know that person too. Then you have two banks with relationships.

#4

I WAS ON MY OWN
Barbara A. Mather
Founder, Mather Consulting Group, Inc.

I was an executive at a *Fortune* 500 company for over thirty years, having worked there for most of my career. In 1998, I got the "opportunity of a lifetime" to move from the East Coast to California to be part of a new division start-up for the company. Ultimately, it wasn't successful, and the company shut it down after three years. I didn't want to look for another corporate job, and I didn't want to move back to the corporate headquarters (an offer that was made to me). My husband loved his job in Los Angeles, and now my kids were finally settled and had all new friends. I didn't want to leave California. So, I gulped, took the leap, and started my own business. My husband said to "go for it."

I was in shock. I always had many work friends and colleagues. Suddenly they were gone. Being safely contained within a corporate structure for my entire career, my whole support system was gone too. Little things. For example, in my previous life I never had to worry about computer problems, or

Belief in yourself is critical; never give up.

making travel reservations. The company had an entire system to handle everything from purchasing paper clips to repairing copiers to preparing financial statements. I would need to do it all on my own—entirely alone—to start and run my own business! It was incredibly lonely and difficult for the outgoing person I was. My daily contact with colleagues and friends was a thing of the past.

I couldn't show the fear. I put the brave face on for my family. In a corporate setting, I had always been fearless—they only knew me as being the rock that I was for many years. I had to succeed on this new venture!

Over the course of a year, I launched my own consulting business, and it took me that first year to find my first client. At times, I wasn't particularly optimistic and didn't think that I ever was going to do it. I started attending a number of professional association meetings to get known. At the first few events I attended, I was terrified; I didn't even know how to talk to these small-business people! I was so accustomed to a big company with its acronyms and the culture. I had to overcome the fear of the unknown.

Amazingly, I started loving the interaction with - entrepreneurs and meeting those who were running smaller businesses. It is just a whole different energy. However, it took me several months to realize that these entrepreneurs were not potential clients. They had no extra funds, and they surely didn't want to pay for consultants. As much as I enjoyed getting to know them, I realized that I was wasting my time; they were not my target audience.

Fear and doubt crept in. I didn't want to fail. Could I ever find a client out there? I began to doubt my own abilities. I knew I needed to change strategies.

The stubbornness in me came out. There was no way that I was ever going to admit to myself or my family that I had made a mistake. I couldn't—wouldn't—show my family the fear. They had faith in me.

Finally, it hit me. The best companies who could pay for my specialized services were larger companies. I did more research. At my former company, I was known as someone who could get things done. Having performed in a multitude of business functions over the years, I discovered the need to specialize in organizational design, change, and development. I continued networking in more focused professional - associations. Finally, I knocked on the right door. I stayed with the first client for a year and immediately moved on to the next at the end of that year. Success is now a most wonderful thing, and fear is an emotion from the past.

What I learned:

- Belief in yourself is critical; never give up.
- If at first you don't succeed in one direction, change it! Nothing is finite or fixed when starting a new business.
- People you can relate to and enjoy meeting with may never become your clients. If they are not a legitimate target audience for you and do not have the ability to pay for your services, move on—quickly.
- In owning and growing your own business, you can feel very much alone in establishing the business direction and strategies. So, plan to rely on others for advice. Hire a business coach. Ask the experts how they did it. Seek counsel when challenged. You don't have to "go it alone" entirely.
- The rewards are yours and the challenges are yours, but remember, there is no safety net like that you will find in a corporate setting.
- Stay fresh in your field and abreast of all new

trends, adjusting your business accordingly. Otherwise, you might find yourself stagnant and without customers—or worse—with a fear that may just overtake and paralyze you!

Applying the lessons learned to your business:

- Make sure that you have enough money saved or enough money to live on when you start your business. It usually takes longer to generate revenues than you've planned for. Starting a business without cash reserves doubles the stress on you. You have to generate revenues to sustain the business as well as pay your rent, eat, and live.
- Market to potential customers who have a need and can pay for your services. If they need what your business offers but can't pay for it, you will have no customers or many uncollectible receivables.

#5

WE WERE LOSING MONEY FAST
Lamar Lawrence
Partner, TMBG, Inc.

Two of my friends and I bought a tax franchise. We chose this franchise because the start-up cost was something we could handle and it was a business that we could operate.

I wanted to do something outside of my day job that would be an investment in the future. I asked other people to join the team. They did.

My wife wholeheartedly encouraged what I was doing. One of the ways she showed her support was to use her retirement fund for my portion of the business investment.

My partners had more flexibility than I did because part of the agreement was that I would continue to work in my full-time job. One partner is a real estate investor and business owner. Another is retired from the government. They ran the business during the day and I ran it at night.

We went through our first tax season in 2003. Right around April or May, we were trying to decide what we were going to do during our off-season. We had done well in our first season; better than we thought we would do, but less than our optimistic goal. We had never done taxes before and were really nervous about this when we started. However, the advertising the franchisor suggested worked and we were doing well.

We had money in the bank. We could pay off the rest of our bills the rest of the year if we shut down. But we didn't want to shut down. That first year we were operating off adrenaline and emotion rather than logic.

Our thought? We have a three-year lease on our space and we need to do something to pay the lease expense, since there wouldn't be any tax revenue coming in the door.

So, thinking that another business would be just as

good, we started a check-cashing business that we thought complemented the tax business. Wrong. We quickly found out it wasn't the same. Before we knew it, September came and we had only a thousand dollars in the bank. We still had to find a way to pay our overhead for three months until tax season started again.

Fear and uncertainty hit. We were running short of cash and trying to figure out how we were going to manage until the next tax season. I thought we needed to put in more money. One of my partners with previous business experience, Aislee Jackson, said no way. He wasn't putting more gasoline on a losing fire. His point: Why aren't we making money? Why would I put more into something that is draining money with no hope of turning around?

It takes money, time, energy, and a lot of stress to be successful.

We had to find a way to do this without adding more investments. Once Aislee spoke, we all realized that we weren't going to put good money into a bad situation.

We finally turned it around without sinking more money into it. We salvaged what we could from the second business and shut it down.

Making those telephone calls was agonizing. We had to negotiate with our creditors. The two biggest were our landlord and the telephone company. We absolutely needed our space. We absolutely needed our telephone.

We negotiated with our landlord to pay the back rent

during the first few months of tax season. We knew that we would have money then. The telephone company was the same deal. We squeaked by.

By the beginning of the second tax season, we were no longer operating on emotion. We still had to count on personal money to start our advertising. However, this investment was different. Advertising was not throwing away bad money. It worked the previous year and it was good money to bring in sales. We were reputable, we had a couple of people who were confident, and we raised four thousand dollars in private money with very good interest terms. One of our partners put in about three thousand dollars and then we gave him that money back on terms. We paid all the notes back.

The second tax season was also successful. We had learned our lesson. We shut down operations with enough cash in the bank to pay our expenses until the next tax season.

What I learned:

- It takes money, time, energy, and a lot of stress to be successful.
- At times I wasn't sure whether I could make it from day to day. Having partners helped.
- Facing failure was a good test of my faith and probably made me stronger. You find out a lot about yourself. Strong faith in God helps.

Applying the lessons learned to your business:

- You have to make the tough decisions. If your business is losing money with no realistic chance of earning a profit and generating cash, then you must close it. If you find that you are losing two cents for every dollar that you generate, that means the more sales you make, the more you lose. Increasing the sales volume on a losing business just makes the losses bigger. You'll soon find yourself in a position where cash is going out the door much faster than it is coming in the door. Unless you have an unlimited source of cash, you must close the business.
- An outsider can often see things that you can't. Rely on advisors to help you see "the forest through the trees." They can also help you make the tough decisions.

#6

WE POURED FUEL ON THE FIRE
Frank Schimicci
CEO, Ioline Corporation, Woodinville, WA

I am not your typical entrepreneur. I came from a *Fortune* 50 company. I was regularly committing and overseeing $100 million in expenditures.

At forty-two, I was running a company subsidiary very successfully. I said to myself, "If you think you are so great, let's see if you can do it on your own." I decided to buy a company.

A friend and former staff member was the general manager for Ioline. He called me out of the blue one day and invited me to dinner. At dinner, he asked if I would be interested in buying Ioline. I was curious why he didn't buy it. His comment was that he couldn't afford it.

I said I wasn't interested. Yet, he convinced me to look at the deal anyway. After I reviewed it, I really wasn't interested. It was almost bankrupt. The previous year the company lost $800,000 and the year before that it lost $400,000.

After a lot of convincing, I finally talked to the staff, reviewed their plans, and wanted to know how the company was going to get to their rosy projections when they were almost bankrupt. It was an industry I knew nothing about. I turned it down again.

Finally, they asked me to make them an offer. I did and they accepted it. The deal closed on March 22, 1992. I bought it ten days before the end of the first quarter. The company reported a $188,000 loss. The following month, the company lost an additional $148,000. I was thinking this might be the worst investment that I ever made. It was a company that was short of going under and it was my money. I did get some outside investors because I decided I did not want to put everything into a company. A small group of silent partners believed in me.

It was worse than I even imagined. Our quality was poor. We had to build two products for every one that was sold. We were competing in markets we shouldn't have been in.

I wasn't stressed. I concentrated on what had to get done rather than focus on the emotion of stress. From my perspective, the name of the game was niche markets. Don't compete against the really big companies who can put you under. Build high quality products. Make it easy to operate and provide great customer service.

We weren't doing that. I wanted to build products that were as easy to use as a toaster. I put a toaster in the lobby. The employees got the message. But first, I had to stop the bleeding.

By the middle of 1992, we were overdrawn on our line of credit, so we decided we had to put more cash in the company. I wrote a check. The investors wrote a check. We poured fuel on the fire. At the time, it felt like wasting good money in a bad situation.

I wrote off $545,000 in bad debt expense. The corner offices went. Cubicles came in. I hired a whole new staff, very selectively. I tried to talk people out of coming to work here. I told them this was a company where you are not going to make the most money. It is a hands-on operation. If you want to be involved in everything and if you want to see the merits of your work, then this is the right company for you. But if you are looking for staff, ego trips, or political agendas, you won't get that here. So, the employees who came to

Ioline were the ones that wanted to be there. The company got great employees that understood what we were trying to accomplish and understood the value of a dollar.

I made everyone understand right at the beginning that if we were going to survive, we had to watch every dime. I walked around manufacturing and collected a bag of nuts, bolts, and cables. I asked, "Who would like twenty dollars?" Everyone raised their hands. I showed them the bag. They got the message.

We thoroughly examined all of the products we produced. We discontinued some. We redesigned other products. I watched every penny. I signed off on every expense...even if it was fifty dollars. I painted the walls with other employees. I thought to myself, "Imagine a *Fortune* 50 guy painting the walls!" We did what it took to get the company profitable.

By the end of the first year, we managed to overcome the early year losses and make a small profit. In year two, we cut 40 percent of the employees, redesigned the core product line to eliminate 50 percent of the parts, reduced cost,

> *Don't ask employees to do what you are not prepared to do yourself.*

and increased quality. We still lost money that second year (1992). The third year, we reduced 40 percent of the space; we earned $27,000. In 1994, profits exceeded $800,000, and by 1995, $1,540,000. We doubled the output of the company by 1997. The company has been profitable twelve of thirteen years, including a run of fifty-three straight months.

I did this using basic business practices: look at all the people, prioritize, plan, execute, get good employees and empower them to do the job, build good products, and be ethical. In 1994, we paid out profit sharing and paid it out ever since with the exception of one year.

Only six of the original ninety employees are still working with me today. The manager who asked me to buy the business is gone. I turned Ioline around. I would not go back to work for a *Fortune* 50 company today.

In 1996, I was nominated for Entrepreneur of the Year. In the past thirteen years, the investors have had an annualized return of 33 percent—not bad for a company that was on its last legs. Despite the initial horror, it turned out to be one of the best investments I've ever made.

What I learned:

- Anticipate the worst. When they gave me the forecast, I looked at it, I cut it down substantially, and we still didn't meet it.
- Stay with the plan and don't stray from it. Stick to the basics. It was worse than I thought it would be.
- Don't get stressed. Address the problem. Look at the logic of the situation and get done what needs to get done.

- Always think of how you can improve the company, how you can make it better, and how you can cut costs.
- When things are going well, try not to think that things are going well. If you do, you may start doing stupid things like making expensive development expenditures or trying to do something you know nothing about.
- Be straightforward, communicative, and ethical with everybody.
- Use walk-around management.
- Don't ask employees to do what you are not prepared to do yourself.
- Make it a point to understand the industry and customer you are serving.

Applying the lessons learned to your business:

- When you are in a tight cash position, you must watch every penny that comes in the door and goes out the door. It is your responsibility to go over every invoice and sign every check.
- Do some research to find out where you can compete in the market. Trying to compete against the market leader can be done. However, it takes a lot of time and dollars. It is much less expensive to find a niche that the market leader doesn't want and be the leader in that niche.

- Communicate with your employees regularly. They have a sense that the business is doing well or is not doing well. If you are honest and ethical with them, they will often give you ideas for improvements and help solve the issues you are facing.

#7

THE "TRUSTED" BOOKKEEPER
Anonymous

About six years ago, we hired an assistant bookkeeper. She was in her fifties with no kids, and her husband was a "DOT engineer." She did not need insurance, didn't need to work, but did it because she wanted to. She said she liked accounting, crunching numbers. She was a dream employee! Jane (not her real name) turned into a mother of sorts for the guys, making sure they took care of themselves. She would often bring in cakes and pies given to her at church. She was a part of our family. She had some serious physical ailments, and we would take her to the doctor. After about three years, she took over accounting completely. She didn't keep a very neat checkbook, but she was watching it like it was her own, so we were okay. Accounting was one thing we didn't have to worry about.

In June of 2002, we discovered that over the past two and a half years since Jane had taken over full control of accounting, she had forged $180,000 in checks. We never knew it. We were in shock. Jane was the last person on earth we would ever suspect of doing something like this. She was the little old lady with a cane, literally.

Also, we discovered we were way behind on our bills (which she quit paying to have more for herself). Before, when vendors would call us about payment, they asked to speak to someone in accounts payable. Who was in charge of accounts payable? Jane! She would make up something to tell them. Again, we were in the dark and never knew we were behind.

You may think, "That would *never* happen to us!" Sure, it can.

We thought we were being careful. Before I signed any checks, I would look over the supporting documents. Before I got those bills, our service manager checked pricing. The service manager and I bled over every bill before it was paid.

Our CPA comes in periodically, but his job is primarily to make sure debits equal the credits, pay taxes, etc. Jane was creating phony invoices to cover the dollars taken. If she took $5,000, then she might assign $2,000 of that to parts, $3,000 to equipment. The CPA assumes the information he is given is legitimate, unless you want to pay for a full audit, which we didn't think we needed. The bank didn't ask for one. The CPA won't question whether a Home Depot bill is really the company's Home Depot bill. Since nearly all the checks were to vendors, her family's vendors, nothing looked out of the ordinary.

Our financials weren't looking that good, but we had excuses: The previous fall we hired several servicemen in anticipation of growth. The next summer turned out to be a total bust. We were overstaffed, but we kept everyone on. In addition, the economy was in the dump. Then 9/11. With all we read in the paper, we were just happy to be in business. Also, during this time we switched accounting software. When something looked out of kilter, Jane would blame the service software not communicating with the accounting software. She could doctor things up. Now when we look back, we realize it was a bunch of smoke and mirrors.

> *Never totally trust your bookkeeper.*

Multiple signatures on a check mean nothing. We don't use multiple signatures, but if we did, she would have signed both! With the millions of checks that go through banks daily, there's no way to verify signatures. Signatures are meaningless.

Fortunately, she never had check-signing privileges. If she had, there may have been nothing we could do. The law doesn't state you have to spend your money wisely. A bookkeeper should *never* have check-signing privileges.

Today, when that envelope comes in containing cancelled checks, I open it. I look at whom the checks were to, and I look at the signature. In fact, all our banking matters now come across my desk first. Sealed. We pay all of our bills online now. Very seldom do we ever write a check.

Our case is thirteen months old now. The civil case is over, and she's supposed to pay the money back. I doubt we'll ever see a penny. On the criminal side, the case has only now been handed over from the detective to the DA. I have doubts it will ever go to court. So, for us this was a big and expensive learning experience. And with all the attorney's fees, it's continuing to cost us. To date, she has never been arrested. If she had stolen a VCR from a retail store, she'd already be serving time.

My guess is most companies out there are like us, and can be taken advantage of very easily. Maybe our experience will help someone else.

What I learned:

- Bookkeepers should not sign checks.
- Don't accept excuses when financial statements are not on time. That's why you hired your bookkeeper. Look at your financial statements when you get them. If something looks wrong, it probably is. Get to the bottom of it.
- Owners have to open bank statements first.

Applying the lessons learned to your business:

- The job of a good embezzler is to become the trusted bookkeeper. Never totally trust your bookkeeper.
- Discovering that someone stole money from you is a shock. Do an audit immediately to find out the real situation.

- Make sure that you press charges against the thief. If you just fire that person, it is likely that the person will do the same thing at another company.
- If you find that vendors weren't paid, apologize and pay them or set up a payment plan if you can't pay the entire invoice.

#8

MY MANAGER QUIT AND TOOK THE DEPARTMENT EMPLOYEES WITH HIM
Anonymous

My father started a small plumbing company and grew the business to approximately $500,000. After college and experience working for a bank, I decided to join him with the purpose of growing the company. I built it to over $15 million. Along the way I learned many valuable lessons in working with people. The story here was probably the most expensive.

One of the ways that I grew the business was to add another division that served our customers' heating and air-conditioning (HVAC) needs. This was a natural addition because we were installing plumbing in new houses and it wasn't that difficult to install the heating and air conditioning in those new houses too. Our builders liked dealing with one company for two trades (plumbing and HVAC) and the business grew rapidly.

Finding people who were willing to work hard and who did quality work was difficult. It was especially challenging in our service department, where we maintained and repaired the equipment we installed as well as replaced old equipment. Our service technicians were in our company trucks working in many different houses and I couldn't watch them. I had to learn to trust that, through training and follow-up, they would do the right thing with our customers.

One of the first service technicians I hired was John (name changed). He took care of our customers well and learned quickly. I was pleased and watched his progress in the early years. John became an outstanding technician.

Our reputation spread and the service department grew to eight technicians. It was time to hire a service manager since my time managing the service department was limited. I still had to oversee the construction departments and run the business. Who better to promote than John?

John jumped at the chance. In the beginning everything was great. The technicians liked him and the department grew to ten technicians. Within a year the problems started. He wasn't doing the management things that needed to get done. Discipline? Forget it. He was the technicians' friend. Numerous meetings and conferences with John did not help. He wasn't a manager.

I realized John was a technician with a manager's title. However, I rationalized that having someone in the service department was better than having to run it myself since I didn't have time to do it.

One day John told me he was leaving. I was relieved. However, that relief turned to anger and shock when eight of the ten technicians left with him. I was left with the two newest technicians who had the least training. In an instant we went from a department with ten technicians to a department with two technicians.

It was summer…a time of year when it was impossible to find technicians. Everyone, even the bad technicians, was working. We were reduced to "putting out fires." The two technicians who stayed worked day and night trying do the work of ten people. They took care of emergencies first; then maintenance when they could get to it. On top of that, they

Employees must understand that the customers, not the manager, write their paychecks.

didn't have the experience to quickly diagnose and repair equipment. They had to learn fast! I made the decision to continue training, even though we were swamped with work. This was the best way I knew to help the two technicians get the information they needed to take care of our customers.

By the end of the busy season, the two technicians who stayed with the company were exhausted. They had worked night and day, seven days a week taking care of our customers. As a result of this crisis, they became much better technicians.

Somehow we got through the summer without losing many customers. We were honest and told them when we could get to them. Some chose to find other contractors. However, most appreciated our honesty and waited until a technician was available, even though they were uncomfortably hot in their houses, and stuck with us.

In the fall I began to find some additional technicians. We still had a lot of work and many other contractors were slowing down. Word spread that we had work. Even though many technicians applied, we didn't hire many of them. We checked references and picked only those who would take care of our customers.

The focus on quality and customer service continued through the rebuild and still continues today. It took four years to rebuild the department to the size it was when John walked out with eight technicians.

What I learned:

- Just because someone is a good employee it doesn't mean that he will make a good manager. The skills to manage work are different than the skills to perform work.
- I waited too long to fire John. I didn't have his replacement so I put up with a bad situation.
- During difficult times, if you are honest with customers and do what you say you will most will stay with you.

Applying the lessons learned to your business:

- Finding good managers is difficult. Many current employees aspire to be managers, but they don't realize what it takes to be a good manager. If they can't do the job, you run the risk of losing a good employee and destroying a department. Find a way that they can manage on a trial basis (i.e., two weeks or a month). They have to do the duties they would on a permanent basis. Many find out what management is really like and prefer to not have the headaches.

- Even when you bring a manager in, you have to keep in touch with the employees. They must have input from you as the owner. Make sure the employees feel that they are working for a great company. Employees must understand that the customers, not the manager, write their paychecks. This way, even if the manager leaves, they should stay because the company is a great place to work.

#9

WE WERE SIX WEEKS AWAY FROM CLOSING
Anonymous

It has been interesting to discover how things work out. Timing has definitely been a key. We started the company in early 2001, one of the worst times for technology companies. It was just the two technical founders and me. I remember having lunch with them and saying, "Guys, we couldn't start a company at a worse time. If we can make it through the next several years, we have a really good chance of being successful in the long term."

It's three years later. We are not out of the woods, but we are starting to see the light at the end of the tunnel, which is very encouraging.

We have thirty people, we have raised several million in venture capital, and probably will raise another significant amount of money in the next twelve months. However, during this whole process, at one point we were six weeks away from closing the doors.

The two founders started this business in their homes. They couldn't find technology that they needed, and decided to write the software themselves. So, they quit their jobs and started developing what would be the genesis of our product suite. For a year and a half, they did consulting work to keep themselves fed. They got the first version of the product built and said, "Now what?"

That's when I came on board. They were looking to raise money and I was looking for another start-up opportunity. We generated $500,000 in revenue and broke even our first year in business. The problem was that at the end of the year, we had no more consulting work and we hadn't made any product sales. We were six weeks from closing the door.

As things go, we were introduced to a gentleman who had just sold a high-tech company, made a lot of money, and fortunately knew something about what we were doing. He knew the position the company was in and could have asked for the world. He didn't take advantage of us.

> *We sacrificed control of our dream to see the dream come to fruition.*

He said, "With my investment, let's take the next year to figure out where we sit in the marketplace, who our competitors are, what the barriers are to entry, and put together a business plan. Let's see if we can raise a round of venture capital money."

That's exactly what we did. In late 2002, we raised our first venture round. The goal was to see if we could validate the marketplace. We wanted to see if we could go sell this product.

Realism hit hard. In the venture capital world, I was a nobody. When you are small with an unproven market, unproven technology, and a few customers, venture capitalists are looking for someone in the company that they can take a bet on. What experience do they have building a high-tech company? Have they made money in the past? It was a sobering experience.

I was no longer head of the company. The first investor who put up the funding became our new CEO. He'd been successful before and was a known entity in VC circles. Part of the venture capital agreement was that he had to be CEO. The venture capitalists were counting on him to do it again.

At the point in time when the venture capitalists came in, we had about seven people working for the company. Now we have thirty. We probably will generate several million in revenue this year with about 70 percent license sales and about 30 percent professional services. We have hit our revenue objectives each quarter and we are happy with our progress.

Would we be here without the venture capital? No. We sacrificed control of the company and swallowed a lot of pride. We sacrificed control of our dream to see the dream come to fruition. This is reality in the world of high technology.

What I learned:

- Never turn down money. Once someone offers the money, you find a way to make it happen. You make a lot of sacrifices. It is a bitter pill to swallow.
- A lot of entrepreneurs come into things naively.

- The world is not black and white. It is shades of gray. You make that adjustment as you grow and mature. Once you realize that, you learn to adjust your thinking and your expectations.
- You need to have very realistic expectations. You will be forced by the venture capitalist world to do this, which can be difficult. You still hold your optimism, but the reality of control, how much control you have, how much control you have in the future, the control of the company and its direction, how rich you may be some day, etc., gets readjusted very quickly.

Applying the lessons learned to your business:

- You have to have customers. A great idea is just that, an idea. Few investors take chances on ideas (and those that do require control). They want to see that the idea is profitable. Find customers who will buy your product at a profitable price and you'll have a better chance of getting funding. In addition, customers bring cash flow to operate the business.
- To see your goals achieved, sometimes you have to adjust your thinking and activities. If "Plan A" doesn't work, try "Plan B." It is very rare that the first plan for achieving the goals gets you where you want to go.

#10

I WAS THRUST INTO ENTREPRENEURSHIP
Doug Kruse
CEO, *Big on Leadership*

I started this business nine weeks ago. I'm still excited. However, these past nine weeks have been like an emotional rollercoaster of euphoria when a deal closes and occasional terror when a "done deal" is cancelled. Here's how I got the opportunity to pursue my own business.

I am an expert at training managers and facilitating dysfunctional management teams that want to "work and play nicely with others." I had twelve years of proven results as a manager, trainer, and facilitator. I wanted to be on my own training and speaking. I told my former boss, Ray, what my dream was. Because I opened my mouth, he had an easier decision in a difficult situation when course enrollments fell off at his education center. When it came time to cut the budget, he called me in and said something like, "Here's your severance package. Now you can go out and pursue your dream."

Even though I had an idea that the layoff was coming, the day it happened I was stunned. He wanted me to clean out my desk immediately. I said, "No! I do not want to interrupt my friends' day with that." And, I really did not want them to see me at six-feet-four and 270 pounds, shaved head, goatee and all, with tears in my eyes. They weren't leaving. I was. Why should I create any drama for them with my moist-eyed, wimpy goodbyes? I went home and told Ray I would come back some other time and clean out my desk.

The next Monday, I met Ray during his lunch hour, cleaned out my desk while almost everyone else was at lunch, and didn't have to see anyone. Later, I even sent Ray a thank-you note for handling the situation in a caring and professional way. He sent me a contract to review in case they ever need me to do training on contract.

It finally hit me when I was driving home in my SUV full of boxes and memorabilia. I had to do something about this. I walked in to my banker and told her the story. Help! She refinanced our house, paid off some short-term loans, and cut our

Build relationships with bankers, accountants, and lawyers before you go into business.

monthly payments significantly so that some of the cash-flow stress was off. I still have a mortgage. However, she knew me and knew that I was good at helping dysfunctional management teams. She set up a line of credit. That took more of the pressure off.

I still had to generate cash. Fortunately, I found my first client, Ron, quickly. Eight weeks ago, I had never done a proposal. I knew Ron and told him I worked with broken teams. He asked for a proposal to do a team-building workshop for his sales managers.

"What's a proposal?" I thought. I got what I thought was a proposal together.

I was really proud of myself for bidding the work at $100 an hour. Of course, Ron accepted this price because the experience of having his people trained was as fresh and new to him as it was to me. It was too easy.

Then I showed the proposal to Joe, my trusted friend, mentor, and leadership trainer whose ranch we would be using for the sales team meeting. He looked at it and asked why I bid that price per hour. I didn't know. It seemed like a nice round number and a lot of money. He looked me straight in the eye and said, "You'll be out of business in six months if you keep giving your experience away at that price." He gave me a copy of one of his proposals and his price list. His hourly rate was more than double my rate!

What should I do? Ron had already accepted my price.

Thankfully, Ron is an ethical person, a trusted friend, and can count on me to deliver value for the money. In the car on the way home from the ranch, I honestly told him what my friend said. Without batting an eye, he said, "I don't have a problem paying you that." So, I escaped and learned a lesson.

In days past of working for my former company, I could count on regular paychecks whether I produced or not. Today, if I don't produce, I don't get paid. It's totally up to me.

What I learned:

- Send out a proposal a day. This goal allows you to have a good chance of generating work.
- Join the associations where your potential clients are. Volunteer for the membership committee. Meet the new members. Your business will always come up in discussions.
- Build relationships with bankers, accountants, and lawyers *before* you go into business. You'll know whom to turn to when the day comes.
- Let people help you.
- Simplifying my life helps me make my company sustainable. I've learned to focus.

Applying the lessons learned to your business:

- A business plan that states the company's overall goals is critical. However, you need to break those goals into activities that you can do every day to reach the goals. Check them off as you accomplish them.
- Your banker, accountant, attorney, and other professionals can help you. Consider establishing an advisory board with these professionals as members of the board. Meet at least quarterly to review goals, accomplishments, and areas where you need help.
- Becoming active in associations will help you with business leads. Volunteering for leadership roles gets your company and you noticed.

#11

I ONLY BROKE DOWN TWICE
Anonymous

I was the general manager of the restaurant for two years, and had worked for the original owners for seven years. I always felt like it needed someone who really cared about the business. Even though I have a degree in chemistry, I fell in love with this restaurant and wanted to own it. I approached the owners. They considered it and they said that I could buy it. That began four months of fear; four months of highs and lows; four months of believing one minute that I'd own the restaurant and the next minute I didn't think I'd ever own it.

The original owners told me that if anybody found out that they were negotiating the sale of the restaurant to me, they would squash the deal. They owned two other restaurants and they were concerned about their reputation. I didn't tell anyone in the city except my fiancé.

I went to a man who doesn't live in the city to help me because I had never bought a business before and I had no idea what to do or how to negotiate it. The yo-yo was getting worse. The owners came up with a different price every day. Another day they would say that I had to put down earnest money. Then, days later, they said there was someone else who was looking to buy the restaurant from them, but they wanted me to have it.

They started pushing. I found out later on that no one else was offering them any money. They were just telling me that so that I would pay them the money for the restaurant.

The reality of the situation was that the restaurant wasn't making any money. However, it was set up in a nice establishment and I knew that I could make it profitable. We had a good base clientele. We just needed to build on it.

They didn't negotiate in good faith. The price that we agreed on included all of the equipment, tables, chairs, decorations, food, and wine. I had to go to the landlord to convince him to continue leasing the building to me. It turned out that everything that was in the restaurant (all the equipment, tables, and chairs—everything) belonged to the landlord. The people that had previously owned the restaurant had gone out of business, so under his contract, he was able to keep everything that was there. So, what I thought I was getting didn't really belong to me.

I was still the general manager of the restaurant. That was my biggest mistake. I kept running the restaurant and trying to finish negotiations at the same time. It was so frustrating. I had to keep a happy face even when I was tense, tired, and stressed out.

Once I knew that I was going to buy the restaurant, I had to get all of the necessary licenses and permits. With a restaurant, there are a zillion things that you have to do and none of the offices are near each other. There is no checklist that anyone gives you that says, "Here is what you need to do to buy a restaurant." So, I would go downtown and get stopped from completing one task because I needed to do something else first; for example, I couldn't get some of the permits I needed because the restaurant was already in existence. One of the licenses, the liquor license, was critical to our business because of the wine that we served. I couldn't get it. The owners of the restaurant owed a fine that they wouldn't pay. I had to drive to our state capital, three hours away, to talk to the people there face to face to resolve that one.

I can hardly convey everything that I was doing; it was literally taking all day long. I'd get up at seven in the morning, drive around the city all day, and come into work at night. I had to put on a face as if everything were normal. It was difficult trying to hide the meetings, the documents, and all the things I was trying to do from the employees.

I had worked with the owners and staff for seven years, so I really trusted them a lot. That was another mistake. Part of me thinks that they wanted to keep it that way so they could control the situation.

The week before I was to take ownership, I wanted to go out to Napa Valley. I didn't want to own a restaurant that prided itself on serving Napa Valley wines without having been there.

While I was there meeting all of the owners of the different wineries, I got a call from my manager. One of my key cooks had gotten into an argument with the owner and had walked out. On top of that, I had gotten a letter from the liquor licensing board in the mail, and she wanted to know if she should open it. I said yes. They were denying my liquor license once again. This was two days before I was supposed to take ownership of this restaurant. We were known for our wine list and could not have wine to sell.

At that moment, I broke down. My fiancé had never seen me like this. He had never even seen me cry in eight years, so he really freaked out. I almost passed out. In fact, he has a picture of me screaming at him, telling him I couldn't go to dinner. I didn't have time to go to dinner. I don't even have a liquor

> *I learned the restaurant business by working for the restaurant first.*

license and my cook that I've depended upon has left. I just wanted to move to Australia and not do this any more.

I was crying so hard that I passed out or fell asleep on a hammock. When I woke up, my fiancé told me he had changed the dinner time and had cancelled all my appointments the next day.

Later, the manager called back to say that the cook called to let me know he would be there for me on Monday morning. He had an issue with the former owner, not with me or with the restaurant.

The reason why I couldn't get my liquor license was because the former owner had not paid that fine. So, in addition, when my manager called me back, she said that the former owner would pay the fine.

When I flew back into town and came in to the restaurant, there was hardly any food left in the whole place. The former owner had gotten so greedy. He had taken a little bit from the restaurant every day and by the time I got back, there was nothing there. I could not believe that someone I had liked and helped build up his other businesses could steal from me.

Then I was standing in front of the liquor licensing board to make sure that I had my licenses. The woman said, "We don't have you on record for any of this." I said, "What do you mean? I have this huge folder and I've done this, this, and this."

There was one more list they hadn't given me. I had to go to eight more places and get signatures. I had to have ten signatures from people who lived in a three-mile radius of my restaurant saying it was okay to sell beer at the establishment.

I almost passed out. I guess the lady saw the look on my face. All the blood just rushed out of me and my eyes swelled up with tears because I was already nuts anyway. All of a sudden, a man said, "Are you [name withheld]?"

I turned around and said yes. He said that he heard that I bought the restaurant. By this time, we had put a notice in the newspaper.

The liquor license board lady then said, "I love your restaurant and you do such a good job." I still had to get the list done. But the incident had stopped me from fainting in front of the license board.

I left there to go and get my food permit. My car almost got towed because I was parking in the wrong place. At that point, I just thought, "I can't do this anymore." I was crying. I was so emotionally drained from it. I didn't know how I was going to take one more step. I had already gone through four months of negotiations and doing all the things that I was supposed to do. I felt like I couldn't even take another breath.

I was driving down the street, angry. The traffic was awful. I was cussing everybody. I was yelling in my car.

All of a sudden, something hit me. I immediately stopped yelling. It was a thought. It was so profound that I shut up.

Here's what went through my head: I'm so glad I have these problems. I'm about to get my very own restaurant. I realized at that point that it was okay. I would get through all of this. I'm able to do it and I am so proud of myself. I'm proud to have these problems because if I didn't have these problems, I wouldn't be getting my own business.

I had come such a long way to realizing my potential. It was all worth it because I was getting the restaurant. All the fear, worry, and uncertainty that I had gone through for the past four months prepared me for ownership.

I haven't had a major bump in the road since. Nothing could match the hell that I went through for those four months. The kitchen could catch on fire now and I would be calm and rational, and able to handle it with no problem.

What I learned:

- I realized that I was lucky to have the problems that I did. That's how I handle things now. When I get mad about something or someone doesn't do what they are supposed to do, I step back and think, "As an owner, these are some of the issues I have to deal with." Now when I want to make a decision and I want to change something, I just do it. If it's not working, then I just change it.
- I should have resigned from the position of general manager while negotiating the buying of the business.
- I learned the restaurant business by working for the restaurant first. This has helped me be profitable because I learned the numbers backward and forward.
- I have a great love of food and wine. I'm just passionate that I have all of it right now. I've got the passion for the customers. I've learned a lot about how to train employees and all the things you go through. With the experiences I had in buying the restaurant, I know that I can handle anything that comes up.

Applying the lessons learned to your business:

- Getting experience working for the type of business you want to own can be critical to your success.

You'll encounter the types of problems that you will have when you own your business in that industry.

- If you don't have experience, then hire a general manager who has proven, successful experience in your industry. This person can help prevent costly mistakes.

- Realize that your experience dealing with issues will enable you to handle whatever comes up. The more experience you have, the less emotional and more logical you will be as critical situations arise. You gain confidence through experience.

#12

WE TRUSTED THE WRONG PEOPLE
Anonymous

I'm the third generation of business owners in my family. My grandfather had a chain of five showerhead distributors from the late 1960s to the 1970s. After my dad couldn't get a job anywhere, he started working for my grandfather. While working for his father, he found a niche in the showerhead industry and started developing a few products. As he was starting, he hired the wrong person to help him develop the products. This person copied all of the files, including vendors and contacts, and opened up a competitive operation. It became very competitive, and finally my dad forced his former employee out of business. My dad would make the same mistake again and it cost him dearly.

My dad continued to grow the business and bought out his father's distributors. Unfortunately, his father sold the name of the company, and as a result, sold the trademark. He learned very quickly that you have to put your trademark in your name. If not, once the trademark is sold, your asset is sold. To continue growing, my father started developing another specialty niche of showerhead products.

Earlier in the company history, my father hired a person at age sixteen who grew to become the CFO of the company. He trusted him and felt he was a partner. He gave him 20 percent equity in the newly formed specialty niche of products. Since my dad trusted him as the money man, he didn't question when the CFO started manipulating money and sucked the cash flow out of the established profitable product line that he didn't own. He wanted to make his own line look good. During this manipulation, my father also hired a product development expert and gave him 10 percent in the new line. The two got together to the detriment of my father.

By this time, I had graduated college and was working full time for the company. At this time, we had a growth decision to make. There were many similar and much larger competitors. The product development expert and the CFO thought we needed to grow dramatically, particularly in the new product line.

In reality, our business model didn't support the growth because overhead became too expensive. As a result, the company started having a severe cash crunch because we were developing too many new products at once. One of the statements I made to the product development man was that it wasn't that we developed bad products; it was just that we developed too many markets at once and our logistics were not in place.

All the growth was done under the assumption that at some point, we would explode and the growth would put equity into the operation. We couldn't get investment capital because there were two competing operations, the ones that my father owned and the one that the CFO and product developer had a piece of. Internally no one wanted to merge the companies. There was too much conflict of interest. As a result, the vendors were not being paid while we were expanding.

Family businesses can be challenging to operate when you cannot separate family issues from work issues.

The expansion discussion continued at board meetings. At one board meeting, I remember distinctly that the CFO said, "Yes, I have the money to continue to develop new products, and yes, I have the financing." My father had no reason not to trust him.

The reality was that the CFO didn't have the money or the funding. He was lying and he just kept pushing it back. My dad fired him in 1985. He felt as if a family member had betrayed him. After all, my father hired him as a warehouse person when he was sixteen. The CFO grew in responsibilities and had helped the company grow.

It was like living through a bad, spiteful, mean-spirited, expensive divorce. The CFO wanted to destroy my father. I was a part of the shareholder's dispute, and even though I didn't have final decision responsibility, he sued me too. Because of the legal battles and shareholders dispute, we couldn't get any more funding. The legal battles lasted for nine years and a $150 million company imploded into bankruptcy. My father filed personal bankruptcy. The company no longer exists.

What I learned:

- I would do it again. As horrible and brutal as it was going through it, the learning experience was incredibly beneficial. Now I am consulting with major manufacturers and even family businesses. I am dealing with other companies that are smaller and who want to grow. Even though I look like I am twenty-eight, my perspective is of a person in his fifties because of what I went through. It really helped me in working with my clients. It shows me a human element of people and it has actually refined how I manage people and projects. I would have been making the same mistakes I am helping them avoid if I hadn't been through this.

- My relationship with my dad is better now that I don't have to look at him every day and there is not so much tension. He is now consulting in the industry again.

Applying the lessons learned to your business:

- Trusting the right people is difficult. Even when a person has grown with your company, he may have grown to a position where he is no longer effective. Coming to this decision can be a shock. However, if the business is to survive for the long term, do not hesitate to replace this person. Find the right person who can do the job at the level it has grown to.
- You must constantly oversee the cash, sales, and profits of your company, even if someone else has the day-to-day responsibility for it.
- Family businesses can be challenging to operate when family members who work together cannot separate family issues from work issues. If you find yourself in this trap, seek professional help from coaches who specialize in family business issues.

#13

I HAD NO CREDIT
Kitty Ariza

I had been selling bridal gowns on consignment from my home and was getting very busy. Why not open a store? In 1995 I did. I had a thousand dollars, a dream, and a friend who was going to be my partner. My friend was a balloon and floral decorator and would handle that end of the business.

We found an industrial location, so the rent wasn't high. I didn't have the credit that I desperately wanted. I couldn't purchase new gowns, so I thought that we would continue the consignment activities that were so successful from my home.

My friend said, "Between us we can afford it. You do the bride stuff and I'll do the decorations." We opened the store. During the first month we were in business, she came to me and said, "I can't afford to do this," and bowed out.

My husband told me that if I wanted to do this, I had to handle it because he wasn't putting any money in it. I was horrified, but I made it. To make matters more frustrating, my husband had super credit and I had none. I needed—no, craved—my own credit. I built and sustained the business for four and a half years, paid all my bills, and got it.

I dealt with the fear a day at a time. Every month was scary as to whether I would make it. Somehow, someone would come in with a big order and save me.

Since we were a consignment shop not in a retail space, I did most of the selling by appointment. Often someone would call and say, "I'll be there in fifteen minutes." If I wasn't at the store, I'd have to rush to get there and sometimes the person wouldn't show up. It was so frustrating! I limped along for six months. I quickly learned that a shop was definitely not the same as having a business in my home. With only word-of-mouth referrals, no advertising, and no drive-by retail location, business was slow.

I got lucky six months later. A newspaper reporter called me. She was interested in me, my shop, and the stories behind some of the gowns. The article appeared in the Sunday living section of our newspaper. My phone rang off the hook.

> *You can get what you want if you persevere.*

That was my savior. I wasn't open to the public. I was in the back of an industrial space. However, I was in the phonebook and people called for directions. I was finally making regular appointments.

Now I had to work on my credit. I wanted to add new gowns. Every time I wanted credit from a company, they asked which manufacturers were currently supplying me credit. No manufacturer was. Not one company was willing to be the first to give me credit.

After much searching and many no's, I found a company at a bridal show that was starting up. They were like me! I asked for, and got credit. Finally! That was my entrée into the world of my own credit rating. Once I got my first credit and paid my bills, it was easier. I found a second, a third, and finally the manufacturers were extending me credit to buy inventory. I had reached my goal.

Soon after reaching my goal, David's Bridal came into my town. They were in a retail location, running a lot of advertisements, and getting the business. I didn't want to compete with that, so I made the decision to close the shop after four and a half years in business.

What I learned:

- You can get what you want if you persevere. Find a way around the no's.
- Credit is very important. It has helped me immensely in the endeavors that I've had since the bridal store.

Applying the lessons learned to your business:

- Establishing and maintaining good company credit is critical for the growth of your business. Initially you may decide to work with vendors who are slightly more expensive, but will extend you credit. This could be critical when you need credit in future years.
- New competitors in your geographic area can be a threat to the survival of your business. If the competitor is a nationally recognized, established business you need to find a way to compete. It might

be to find a niche that the competitor doesn't attract or to provide services that the competitor doesn't. You could also sell to the competitor or shut the business down. However, you have to do something. If you can't find a way to survive the competition, then you need to find a way to profitably close the business.

#14

I HATED THE BUSINESS I BOUGHT
Jim Annis
CEO, *Applied Staffing, Inc.*

I've bought a business. I've started a business. I ended up hating the business I bought. That's why I started a business after I sold the one I hated. But before I could have a business I love, Applied Staffing, I had to go through the pain of a business I hated.

I had been chief operation officer and president of a large industrial distribution and manufacturing company for about thirteen years. I was making well into six figures for a number of years. I just needed to do something different.

I came home one day and told my wife that I had quit my job. She had an Oreo moment. She left the house, bought a bag of Oreos, came home, and proceeded to eat them. After that, I got her support.

We had to buy a business. I looked around for something, and bought a vending company. I've never had a problem generating the top line; i.e., generating sales.

I bought a vending business that was doing about $200,000 in sales. In my former job as the CEO of the distribution company, the telephone rang constantly with good news: orders, projects, etc. At the vending company, the phone never rang, and when it did ring, it was always a negative call. A coin jammed. Someone didn't get what he or she paid for. Money got stolen. It was very negative. Despite the negativity, I managed to grow the business to $2 million in sales in three years.

Starting out in this business, I was cash poor so I had to depend on the vending machine companies to finance me. They charge you an arm and a leg for that privilege.

You found out that one of the cash guzzlers in the vending business is buying your equipment. It costs $40,000. You bought the equipment because you have a contract from a customer who wants it in his location. The customer changes his mind and cancels the contract. Now you have a $40,000 investment that you are counting on being in a place for five years to pay for the equipment and get a return on your investment...and it's sitting in your warehouse. I absolutely hated it.

I also had a problem with the bottom line because I didn't realize two things. First, there is a huge amount of interest you have to pay to finance the equipment. Second, when you are dealing with that much cash, the banks charge you a huge amount of money to handle the coins. We were paying at least a thousand dollars a month for the privilege of having the bank handle the coins. Since I didn't know the business going in, I didn't know about that. It wasn't in my projections.

When a person called in sick, I went on their routes for them. It was a constant fire drill. Six weeks into the business, I knew I hated it. However, I tried to make it work. I went to a seminar and learned that you take that negative phone call and turn it into an opportunity. Convince your client why they chose you to be their vendor. That worked for a couple of years.

Buying an existing business can be buying a bunch of other people's headaches.

After the company started growing, I didn't make any extra money because I had to keep buying equipment. In addition, the cash that we had to keep in the machines grew as the number of machines grew. I couldn't make money on it. It had to sit on the machines.

I kept it up another three years. I did some soul searching to find out what I really wanted to do. Soon after, a guy came in one day and wanted to buy the vending company. I practically gave it away. I didn't make any money on the transaction, but I didn't lose any money either.

I found that buying a business is buying a bunch of other people's headaches. I certainly learned a lot in terms of running a business from that business. It helped when I started Applied Staffing; a business that is very profitable and very successful. It's a business I love.

What I learned:

- Sometimes the bad things can teach you what not to do in the future.
- Try to turn the negativity into a positive. If you honestly can't turn it around, then it is time to do something else.

Applying the lessons learned to your business:

- Starting or buying a business on impulse and without research is very dangerous. Work in the business for a while to see whether you like the industry. If not, then don't buy a business in that industry.
- Even if you don't like the business, find a way to make it profitable so that you can sell it. Establish a timeline for the sale and determine how businesses are valued in the industry you are in. Then, work toward creating the largest value you can for your business. You'll get more for the business when you sell it.

#15

I GOT FIRED
Sydney LeJeune
Owner, Office Helper

I was working as a bookkeeper for a company in the late 1980s. I was one of the few people in my community who was computer savvy, plus knew accounting. I worked with the programmers to get all the glitches out of the accounting system.

Within two weeks of me telling the owner that the glitches were gone, he "laid me off" because he didn't think he needed a full-time bookkeeper. To top it off, he did it just weeks before my one-year anniversary, so I couldn't collect unemployment. Then, when he did it, he treated me like a criminal and had someone stand over me when I packed up my personal things.

It was so unnerving. I had never been treated that way before or since. Steam was coming out of my ears by the time I got home. The owner had screwed me over and I was so mad. At home, I said to my husband, "That's it. I will never work for one person."

My husband had been pushing me to go into business. He said that was what we were going to do now. But we still needed my paycheck. I went to work as a temp. I did that during the day and worked my business at night. To get my first customer, we made up some flyers. My husband literally went door to door in an industrial complex. He saw a business owner who was interested. He went back two more times and finally the man agreed to see me on a Saturday. His company had been in business for only six months.

In the late 1980s, home-based businesses were not the norm. He asked me if we owned or rented our home. I told him we were renting at the time. He said that renting a home made him nervous because, in his opinion, there was nothing to prevent me from just packing up and disappearing. I looked at him and I said, "Let me ask you something. What is the difference in renting a home and renting an office, because most people don't own their office space? I am a whole lot more likely to abandon a rented office than I am to pack up my whole family and move."

Success is the best revenge.

He said, "You know, I never looked at it that way before." He hired me and is still my customer, fifteen years later. My husband never went door-to-door selling again. He thought that the one customer he got me was enough.

He actually was right, although it didn't happen as quickly as he expected it to. My first customer referred me to another customer and then another.

Unexpectedly, I got pregnant. Because of pregnancy complications in the past, I was afraid to take on any new customers and build the business. And we still needed my paycheck. I had to continue working for a temporary agency, which I didn't want to do.

When my baby was two weeks old, my girlfriend who worked in the health care industry found a retirement community that needed help with their books. She highly recommended me. I went and talked to them and got that account. It was big enough that I never had to temp again.

From that point, the business grew exponentially. I'm still working out of my house. I've bought a Medicaid and Medicare filing business. I now am the sole breadwinner in our household, since my husband became disabled and can't work.

My stubbornness made me succeed. I think a lot of people would have just given up. But I was determined that since I had started down that path, that was what I was going to do. Success is the best revenge.

What I learned:

- Murphy's Law rules. Plan for the unexpected because that is what is going to happen. If you don't get upset by that and just keep right on going, you will work through the problems. You will prevail. Just don't think it is going to be this easy, magic thing.
- When I started my company I knew how to do bookkeeping, but I didn't know the business of running a business. I read everything I could get my hands on. I paid attention to what I read. Much of the information I learned in my first year has held true all this time.

Applying the lessons learned to your business:

- Always continue learning. One way is by joining associations. You may have a skill that you turned into a business. However, that skill doesn't teach you how to run a business. When you join the associations for your industry, you meet people who can help you run your business. You will see businesses that are doing well that you can learn from. Join a peer group if your association offers them. These groups match company owners of a similar size with similar goals in geographically distant areas. As part of this noncompetitive group, you share the good, bad, and ugly of your business. Everyone shares financial statements and helps each other with their businesses.
- Another way to continue learning is to set aside time every day to read business-related materials or watch business-related programs on the Internet.

#16

THE MARGINS DROPPED TOO LOW
Eric Hansen

I was in the lawn maintenance business and looking to augment my business with a lawn care business. The difference? To put it simply, lawn maintenance includes cutting lawns, while lawn care is fertilization.

I wanted to augment the business in the late 1990s because the margins for lawn maintenance were slipping and the margins for lawn care were great. Lawn care was getting 50 to 60 percent margins and I was looking at 5 to 15 percent margins on lawn maintenance.

I found a lawn care business. The owner was bored with it. He had built the company from scratch to about 125 accounts. It had a great brand and a great trademarked logo. I made a bid for the company and it was accepted.

My thought was, "If I can build this company up, eventually I'll sell off the lawn maintenance. We'll stay in the lawn care because it has higher margins." I put my business plan in place. I started marketing and advertising to increase the business. I added in some trucks and equipment, employees and software systems. I figured we'd be at two thousand accounts within a couple of years. Wrong.

Change continuously.

The company got up to about four to five hundred accounts within the first season. I was on track. Then the bottom dropped out of the economy. Jobs were at stake and people were not spending money unless they absolutely had to. Lawn maintenance was still needed. People didn't want to cut their grass. But fertilization? That can go.

It took its toll on us. The larger companies cut their prices in half. We still managed to get to about six hundred accounts, but the margins eroded. We used to have great margins in fertilization and poor margins in lawn care, and the situation flipped before our eyes.

The company was profitable. But was it profitable beyond our wildest dreams? Was it something that I wanted to replicate all the way from six hundred accounts up to two thousand or more? The answer was no.

Reality was that I didn't like the business enough. I didn't have the passion for it. I didn't say, "Regardless of the profits, I like making lawns green."

There wasn't an ability to want to build it up and it wasn't happening that way. We were spending too much on marketing and not getting enough return.

I had to make a decision quickly. Could I turn the situation around? No. The larger companies could eat me. Even though, in my opinion, I used better chemicals, customers didn't care. They didn't see the difference. They cared about the price.

I had to turn on a dime. I made the decision that it was time to let the giants have my business. I didn't want to and couldn't compete against them.

What were the big guys interested in? Customer contracts. My accounts. So, I went out to gain customers' contracts. The price didn't matter. We gained about one hundred more customers and sold the business to a competitor.

What I learned:

- React to situations as they unfold. Change continuously. We alleviated a lot of the fear because we watched, reacted, and changed.
- Watch your competition. React to what they are doing.
- If you see a profit in the first year or two, it is a gift.

Applying the lessons learned to your business:

- Monitoring your business plan lets you see opportunities and threats before they become major crises. You must act when you see a threat to your business. Pay close attention to your customers. If they stop buying what you are providing, why did they stop? Can you provide a different product or service to those same customers? If the answer is yes, then you found another revenue stream. If not, then you must find new customers or another way to survive.
- Pay close attention to your competition. What type of pricing are they advertising? Can you match that price? If not, then you have to find a way to deliver more value to the customer at the prices that you must charge to earn a profit.
- If you can't find a way to generate and keep customers or "beat the competition," you may want to sell your business to your competition.

#17

I HAD A HEART ATTACK
Mark McGregor

I was stressed out. I had major family problems. I had issues at my construction job. One evening at a hockey game, I had a severe, massive heart attack. It was totally unexpected. I was only thirty-five years old. The only thing wrong with me was a "little" stress. I had no history of heart disease; nor did anyone in my family. It was a fluke.

The heart attack forced me to be on disability for one year. It was that bad.

Before my heart attack, I had an interest in the financial industry and was taking correspondence courses. I started because I had checked out some financial advisors and I didn't like any of them. I thought that I'd do it myself and started taking classes.

During the time on disability, people were coming to me and asking me questions about their mutual funds and retirement funds. I decided that since I was giving this advice for free, I might as well use it to my advantage. I got my license and started a business. I thought that I would reduce my stress as a business owner.

Unfortunately, I learned that the stress of running the business was as bad as the heart attack at times. I found the greatest challenge in my business was the financial aspect. Where's the cash going to come from? It dawned on me that when you are working in construction, you get a regular paycheck every week. If you are sick, like I was, you can get unemployment. When you are self-employed, if you don't work, you don't eat. That was the most stressful part in the change and crossover. My greatest challenge was the fear of the unknown.

So why do I continue? I do it because I can see things. I can make an impact on people's lives. I never did finish my financial certification. I decided to help people in other ways. I wanted to help them reduce their stress so they don't have a heart attack at thirty-five or fifty.

My motivational speaking and training business reminds me of my previous employment in construction. I helped build one of the largest sports arenas in the world. While I was operating that crane, there was a lot of stress.

Build something that has an impact, that you feel passionate about.

When I was done with the project, I could walk away and the building would always be there for many people to enjoy.

When I'm speaking or writing, it is the same thing. People will come to you afterwards and say you had an impact. I feel that I am helping with a different type of a building and I can see the results well after the event.

What I learned:

- Unmanaged stress can kill you. I was lucky. I got a second chance. I'm using it to do what I enjoy in business, despite the financial hardships at times. I enjoy the hours and I can do things that I have to do with my daughter without stress.

- Do something that has an impact, that you feel passionate about. Build something.

Applying the lessons learned to your business:

- If you don't like your business, then find a way to turn what you don't like into something you like. If you can't do this, then it is time to plan your exit strategy. Owning, managing, and growing a business is stressful and takes more hours than working as an employee. You have to enjoy it most of the time and look forward to each day, its challenges, and rewards.
- Get feedback from your customers. They will tell you whether you are serving their needs. If you are, then continue to do it and ask for referrals. Most customers will be happy to refer your company if they are satisfied with your services. If your customers give you negative feedback, ask for suggestions. They usually can tell you what they want. Follow up on those suggestions and turn the negative feedback into positive feedback.

#18

A LARGE COMPETITOR TRIED TO ELIMINATE US

Gordon Kinne

CEO, Med-Pay, Inc.

Med-Pay, Inc., is a third-party administrator (TPA) for companies that self-fund their own medical plan. Our company processes claims and purchases reinsurance to limit catastrophic exposures for our clients. When President Clinton was in office, he proposed the Universal Health Care Plan where a company had to have five thousand or more employees covered to opt out of this program. At that time, our biggest client had about three thousand employees and most of our other clients had a couple hundred employees.

The proposed health care plan was going to legislate our company out of business, so we looked for partnerships with an insurance carrier. We found a company, Humana, and started talking to them. Through negotiations, we ended up selling Med-Pay to them even though Clinton's health care proposal tanked. We still thought that managed care HMOs were going to be the saving grace, and we didn't fit that mold.

We ran our company inside Humana for two to three years. About three years into our agreement, Humana wanted to dispose of the TPA. This gave me the opportunity to buy the company back. I did. However, one of the health care providers that we were contracted with bought the Clinton health care proposal concept hook, line, and sinker. As a result, they bought all their doctors, set up their own insurance company, and tried to block us from buying Med-Pay back since we were their competition.

In fact, they went to all of our customers who were using their doctors and told them that if they stayed with Med-Pay, they would not receive their discounts any more. Some of our customers asked *Do not take business decisions personally.* why, and the health care provider couldn't give a good explanation to any of them. I believe they were just trying to eliminate the competition.

Some of my clients felt they couldn't stay with Med-Pay because they didn't want to cause any turmoil for their employees by changing health care providers. Some of our clients told the health care provider that they were wrong and left them. We then helped them set up contracts with the other hospital in town.

It was an incredibly difficult situation. The worst thing that happened was when we won a government agency contract by being the lowest bidder, and the agency was told by the health care provider that if they wanted to use their network, they couldn't use Med-Pay.

I tried everything. I went to see the new person at the health care provider's location. I told him that all we wanted to do was process claims. We obviously didn't always agree with what they were doing, but we had to be the guardian of our client's dollars. In my opinion, we tried to work with them.

The administrator told me they'd have to just look at each company on a case-by-case basis. I told him that if we were to lose one more piece of business, that we would sue them. I didn't want to do that. However, I was at my wit's end trying to save Med-Pay.

He puffed up and said, "You are going to sue [name withheld]? We are pretty big."

My reply, "We have law firms that have kicked your ass three times already and they'll take it for free. It won't cost me a thing but time to play the game."

I turned the lawyers loose and we solved the situation in seven days. This was after six months of stress and sleepless nights.

This health care provider was just trying to eliminate the competition. We lost between 30 and 40 percent of our business in a short time period. We still prospered, but it was pretty brutal. I aged five years in six months.

What I learned:

- The person who was driving the effort to keep our clients from staying with us lost and took early retirement. We survived. I'm not saying that this one issue forced him out, but it was a big deal and became front-page news in our local newspaper.

- If you are honest with people, treat them fairly, and are up front with them, you will get rewarded more than you get beat.
- Do not take business decisions personally.
- Sometimes, if you know that you are right, threatening a lawsuit is the final silver bullet. You don't want to take it there, but if you can say that you've tried everything else (and I had), you have no other choice. It worked.
- Prayer, spousal support, and some really good friends will help you get through the tough times.
- It was really a good lesson. At first, I was bitter at the companies who left. However, I realized that some just didn't want to be in the middle of a fight. We did survive and have built back the company. Perseverance and trying to do the right thing got me through.

Applying the lessons learned to your business:

- Always be aware of how you are perceived in your community. People want to be treated fairly. If your company is thought of as a bully, then it is very difficult to get rid of the reputation. The press can be your friend in these cases if you are factual with them and you don't try to hide from them when they call.
- Many larger companies will fight to eliminate the competition. You must find a reason that a

customer or prospective customer will benefit more by using your company's products and services rather than patronizing your larger competitor. It doesn't always have to be price. Many times people will pay more if they perceive the value is there for the price they pay.

#19

I GOT SICK AND COULDN'T WORK
Nita Black
President, MO's Memphis Originals

I started a consulting business to write business plans and access capital for small- to medium-sized businesses. I enjoyed it and my customer base was growing rapidly. In 2001, I was working on a large grant to acquire funding for a new markets venture fund. It was pretty exciting, and the deadline was drawing near.

My voice mailbox was nearly always full. I was under a lot of stress, so I started taking a lot of Advil while I was working fourteen to twenty-two-hour days. I couldn't sleep because I was so stressed and excited at the same time. Since I didn't do drugs, smoke, or drink, I thought my health would be the last thing to go.

My friends and family started to get concerned. They saw my health deteriorating. They dragged me to the doctor. I didn't see any need to be concerned as there was "nothing wrong with me." I had work to do. However, thankfully in retrospect, they persisted. It took seven family members and a dear friend to trick me into getting help.

After many tests, I was diagnosed as manic depressive and was hospitalized for a week. My entire life, including my business, came to a halt. The doctors wouldn't give me a date of when or where I could go back into business.

The hospital stay scared me. I realized that there was no one to take over things in my absence. My self-confidence was shot. I felt like the world was ending and I had no purpose. One good thing that happened was I was able to understand how people feel when they are in treatment in a place that seemed like a jail sometimes, with only alcoholics and drug-heads for conversation.

Through this entire time I rested, prayed, and counseled with professionals. Slowly my business and personal lives came back together. I never did finish that grant application.

My business managed to survive. During my yearlong forced hibernation, I found a good alliance with a person whose talents were complimentary to mine. I slowly began to accept more clients and start writing business plans again.

As a result of my business-planning clients, I started another company. I had done research indicating that students' behavior began to change when music and art programs were eliminated from school systems' curricula. I already had existing clients in the music, publishing, and art businesses. I decided to put the two together and market the "invisible" value of art and music. Another research study indicated that behavior is most heavily impacted by the person closest to the individual: a mom, dad, aunt, or caregiver. So, MO's customers are really the "Krispy Kreme Crowd," people aged seventeen to seventy-five.

Much of my strength to do this came from a personal relationship with the Lord. He placed Rick Warren's book, *The Purpose-Driven Life,* in my hands along with many people and prayers. I don't play golf, but have had a few lessons. They say that a perfect shot is when the ball is hit in the sweet spot on the club. I really feel like I am in the "sweet spot" of the Lord.

I knew this company would require some capital. I decided to use part of my retirement funds for this venture. I was "putting my money where my mouth was" since it meant so much to me.

You must have a disaster plan, even if you never have to implement it.

My first advisor said that there would be no tax implications when I used my retirement funds to buy stock in a company I owned. I planned to buy company stock and hold it in my IRA. She was wrong and I am paying the 10 percent penalty because of it. However, I am committed to a business that has meaning for me, as well as others, giving me purpose to my life. The health scare I had made me look at what I really wanted to do and I'm doing it now.

What I learned:

- Your health is critical. If you are totally stressed out, find out what is bothering you before you get sick and can't work.
- Research is critical when you are running your own business. Ask several advisors before you take the opinion of one, and better yet, do the research on your own. Ask for others' advice.

Applying the lessons learned to your business:

- You must have a disaster plan. Hopefully you will never have to implement this plan. However, it is in place if the unthinkable happens. The plan should encompass the activities to occur if your company's managers or you die, get sick, are incapacitated, or disabled.
- Another disaster plan describes what will happen if there is a fire, flood, hurricane, tornado, or other reason that you can't enter your office building. Make sure that you have backups of all computer programs and data off site. Customer lists are critical. If all of the products and services in your building are unavailable, as long as you have your customer list and prospective customer list, you can rebuild the company.

#20

I HAD NO CUSTOMERS
Pauline Cormier

My husband was on strike and I needed a project to keep me busy. I had just received a set of watercolors as a gift. I started to draw and paint a picture of a little girl on a swing. Lying in bed that night, I remembered a promise that I had made to myself when I was five. I was going to write a children's book.

I created a book. My husband helped me create five hundred toy dogs. These stuffed animals accompanied the book and gave children something to focus on while the story was being read. That was the easy part. It was my passion. Now I had to get my passion into the marketplace.

I got my computer, my scanner, my printer, and my fax machine; none of these office tools were familiar to me. I'd never had to use them. Now I did. I felt like a doctor who was going to the hospital to operate with all of the tools he needs but without his license to operate. I had no clue what to do, but I thought if anybody could do it, I could. The determination was there.

I went to the small business department of the Canadian government. One presentation was from an officer in the Royal Bank. She gave us the procedures for getting a loan. She helped me map out my business plan. In my travels, I had seen a sign in a bank that said, "If you're starting a new business, come see us." I thought I would go in for a trial run. I had no expectations of getting a loan. I got it. Now I was on my way.

I started in March 2001, and the books and beagles came to my door on September 11, 2001. It was hard. It was harder than I ever thought. I had to find a market. I needed to earn money to pay the loans.

Find people to encourage you. Negativity brings you down.

I had everything down pat. I had my numbers. I knew exactly what I wanted. But I had no sales. The perpetual optimist in me kept saying, "one small sale at a time."

I didn't get discouraged. However, when I made a sale, as soon as I got the money it was gone. I made a third product: a CD to accompany the beagle and the book. Now I had an even bigger package and even bigger debts.

My husband was very supportive. If it weren't for him, I probably would have given up. I was, and still am, spending more than what I'm making. But he never says, "I want you to quit."

A brainstorm hit. I went to schools for story time. I made the products interactive. Children paint faces on the characters in the book and get a beagle. Dealing with the school bureaucracy is tough. Getting into schools takes a long time. However, I am seeing some progress. The children's faces when they hear the story and see the products keeps me going.

I've been nervous, scared, apprehensive, and excited. It's been an emotional rollercoaster ride.

I finally figured it out. I had to compare my business journey with my wedding night. We've been married for thirty-five years and it is great! I hope I don't have to wait that long to reap the benefits of my business journey!

What I learned:

- Talk with people who have a positive attitude. Find people to encourage you. Negativity brings you down.
- Do what you have to do. I still work two days per week in the beauty salon to pay the loans. It gives me the flexibility to do what I need to do to build the business.
- I like a challenge. I tell everyone I'll be on *Oprah* one day. When you have a goal, you stick to it.

Applying the lessons learned to your business:

- Get help with areas of your business that you don't know how to do. Many experts can help you. You might get the information that you need from seminars and workshops. Other times you need one-on-one consulting with experts in your field. A third option is to find a noncompetitive business and speak with the owner. Many times that person will help you through the tough times by sharing his story of how he got through it.

- Find allied products that you can provide to your customers. Many times this is a quick way to increase revenues. It is much easier to increase the purchases from an existing customer. A new customer is not likely to purchase as much because you don't have a track record with him.

#21

OUR CUSTOMERS DIDN'T SEE WHY THEY NEEDED OUR PRODUCT
Gary Markle
President and CEO, Colorado Springs Technology Incubator

I am a reformed entrepreneur. Between 1979 and 1999, I started three software companies, built them to respectable size, and sold them to publicly traded companies. When the Colorado community I live in decided to create a high-technology incubator, I threw my hat in the ring to be the CEO. Now I can provide experience and guidance to technology start-ups.

Without the help of the government, my first company would not have made it. My first software application company was launched at the same time the IBM personal computer was being brought to market. We developed a banking application that was mainframe oriented and modified it so that it would run on an IBM PC. This banking application forecasted the impact of interest rates on banks' balance sheets, currencies, and other banking activities that are affected by interest rates.

We got into this business in 1979 as a small division of an early stage start-up that was venture funded and eventually bought by Computer Associates. Computer Associates decided that our little niche company didn't fit the overall profile, so we did a leverage buyout with the company. Charles Wang helped us finance the buyout. With six customers, all of the founders "signed on the dotted line" and invested money into the business.

I was about thirty-two years old. I took my life savings of $20,000 and put it into this business. I was single and I thought, "Well, this is my chance." I didn't know what I was getting into. I was a founder of the company and I was in charge of sales and marketing. It was my responsibility to generate revenues. I was the meal ticket.

The problem was that we were a niche company with a neat piece of software that the banks liked but didn't need. Most banks said, "That's a nice thing to have, but I don't have to have it, so why should I buy it? I'm fighting this fire right now, so why don't you call me in six months?"

So I had a great product that banks really needed, but didn't *think* they needed. I had to learn to sell missionary work into a very traditional market that didn't like change and new ideas.

Cash was getting short. There were many times that we issued our paychecks and they sat in the drawers until we had enough funds to pay ourselves. And, to make matters worse, we all had our houses pledged as collateral and had taken a lot of risk ourselves.

We didn't get any venture capital. We did apply and receive a Small Business Administration (SBA) loan. Part of the requirements with the SBA was that the founders could only earn a certain amount of money. They put a limit on our salaries, which was fine with us because at times we weren't getting any salary at all. Our life was very much hand-to-mouth, and we were very close to the flame on several occasions.

We continued through it. There was momentum gathering. We started to turn the corner away from missionary selling with a heightened interest in buying our software. We had to persevere. I had invested $20,000, my life's savings at the time, and didn't want to lose it. All of the founders in this company had been in larger companies, didn't like it, and didn't want to go back. We just decided to hang in there.

We did many things to get rid of the stress. We had a lot of company get-togethers. We tried to identify the specific areas that the people in the company were very good at and try to focus those people on those areas. We tried to take away from them responsibilities that they weren't very good at.

We also had partners that we could rely on. Everybody came to work each day with a strong work ethic and I think that was what got us through. Even during the toughest times, you could look around and see the partners with their shoulders to the grindstone, working late hours. Many of us went on business trips and worked three or four hours on the plane.

Our CEO was a steadying force. I can remember being so stressed out about trying to sell that I called him one time and said, "I can't even remember my phone number." He walked me through this whole thing. He really was a mentor and a person who put a lot of things into perspective for all the young guys in the company who had signed on the dotted line with the SBA loan and who had their houses pledged as collateral for the loan.

You must be the calm force in the face of adversity.

The CEO was the guiding figure and was very important to this company. He didn't get rattled. He didn't get stressed. In hindsight, the kind of things that got us through were his continued belief in the business and everybody's continued belief in our product and what we were doing. There was never a conversation about, "Are we doing the right thing?" or "Do we really have a market here?" We never second guessed ourselves or asked if we should fold the company.

Then the government stepped in and mandated that banks have our type of software. They didn't mandate that the banks buy from us; just that they purchase software like the software we created and sold.

So, we were legislated into business and were very, very fortuitous at the time. This was around 1985 when the prime rate was 12 percent. Our company was the largest in the world in this little niche. We grew to $20 million in revenues and several hundred employees around the world.

What I learned:

- As an entrepreneur, you have to understand what I characterize as your bed partners. You really have to know them because even though you may have worked together at MCI or some other company, the pressures of an entrepreneurial situation start-up are grossly magnified. If you don't understand the personality of the ones you are working with, it is going to be almost a nightmare to get through.
- Pioneer work is tough. If you believe in your products and they are needed, you have to sell their benefits and convince the market of their benefits. The missionary work can't last long if you want to eat.
- You need a calming force, such as our CEO provided for us. When we were really rattled and stressed out, he was there to talk us through it and keep us going.

Applying the lessons learned to your business:

- Always keep abreast of the latest federal, state, and local government regulations. You might find a new law that requires your customers to purchase your company's products. When this happens, you must immediately do the proper advertising and public relations to ensure that your customers and prospective customers are aware of and comply with the law. This brings revenue to your company.

- As the business owner, you must be the calm force in the face of adversity. If your employees see you upset or stressed, they will follow your lead and become worried. In addition, if you see one of your employees worried or stressed, you must talk with that person to see if you can alleviate that worry. Otherwise, that person could become a detriment to your company because the worry could cause his inability to properly perform his duties and negatively influence other employees.

#22

THE GOVERNMENT TAKETH AWAY
Victoria Kamm
CEO, *Thermal Engineering, Inc.*

We are a small, family-owned manufacturing company that has been in business since 1950. In the late 1980s the Environmental Protection Agency (EPA) began talking about enacting the Clean Air Act, which forced the recovery and recycling of refrigerant used in car air-conditioning systems and home air-conditioning systems.

At the time, we could only produce less than a thousand refrigerant recovery units. So, we began discussions about the potential to "gear up" to meet the potential demand. My feelings were to only produce the number we could produce and not gear up. I was outvoted by my husband and his father.

The EPA Clean Air Act was enacted in July, 1990. Even though we geared up, we still couldn't meet the demand. Revenues were increasing exponentially and we were hiring as fast as we could.

Despite the increase in labor and materials, the company could only build six thousand units per year at the end of 1991. I again said, "Don't bother adding more expense to expand." My feelings were that if you are not going to build to what is clearly the demand, then what's the point? I knew that we would never meet the demand.

We knew we could not possibly fill all the orders. There was some thinking that people would cancel and try to get them from someone else. It never happened because no one else could supply them either.

Revenues and profits were great.

On July 1, 1992, the market disintegrated. The EPA said that they didn't have the revenues to enforce the monitoring of refrigerant usage. Sales stopped that day. Six million dollars in orders were cancelled in one day. We were $1.7 million in debt.

We laid off 150 people in one day. We had no choice and it was not fun. What we had built was gone and the people who built it had to go too. We had no other work for them.

The ironic thing is that the EPA said they really regretted that some companies may not survive. We were going to be one of the survivors.

My father-in-law was very clear that we needed to go through bankruptcy. But my husband and I refused to do it. My father-in-law was eighty years old and didn't want to deal with the issues. However, my husband and I needed the business to support our family and our future. We decided that we would pay our suppliers and concentrate on the other parts of the business that were not affected by the EPA mandate. After all, the business was profitable before the EPA and it was going to be profitable again after the EPA, even though we were $1.7 million in debt with millions of dollars of inventory we couldn't sell.

Two months later, we still had suppliers returning equipment. A lot of it got junked, some got sold as scrap, and we still have some of it. Mostly we just wrote it off over the course of years. There was nothing we could do with it because it eventually became obsolete. The suppliers clearly didn't care.

We worked at it. I say all the time that there is something to be said about getting up and going to work. There was only one point where I was really frightened and that was early on when my daughter was eighteen months old. I was thinking, "What are we going to do?" because at that point, my identity was tied up with the company. That was who I was and what I did. It was more frightening to think that I didn't have anything else other than going bankrupt. I just couldn't imagine what else I was going to do. I guess it was just a fear mechanism.

There was a period of time when distributors would call and I'd answer the phone, "Thermal Engineering," and they would say, "Oh, I didn't think you would answer." So I'd ask, "Why are you calling?" Some of our competitors would say they thought we were dead or we were gone and they would call up just out of curiosity.

I kept thinking of the many opportunities that were there for staying in the business. For me the most important thing was to stay in the industry. So, we just decided to do it. Thermal was profitable and always had been. We paid some things off, took losses on our income tax returns, and set up some payment plans. We were on a payment plan with one supplier for ten years. We had purchased from them for our other products

Before you work for the family business, work for another company.

and weren't a new customer. They were just astounded. I'm sure they thought when they set up the repayment plan that we would never survive. Last year we finished paying it off.

We had a couple of meetings with the sales representatives. One wrote me a letter demanding $52,000 and stated that he was going to get an attorney.

I said go ahead and knock yourself out. We had a couple of meetings where the reps thought we were just not giving them money and we screwed them. It was just like our suppliers, they knew we couldn't pay it, but they wanted their money anyway.

Even though we didn't have the money and we weren't a public company, we said, "Here is where we are. Here is our situation. Here is our loss and here is what we are doing to recover." We thought the transparency would be a good thing and it was.

Unfortunately, we had some people still yelling, "You owe me the money." I reminded everyone, including the sales representatives, that we had to sell our other products so that we could get out of this debt mountain. The only way we could pay off the debt was to sell more of our other products.

Many of the representatives left anyway because they didn't believe that we could make it. They didn't want to take the chance to look bad with their wholesalers. We had to have the increased sales to pay them, but they wanted to make sure their customers didn't get mad at them and give them a hassle with the other lines they represented. We changed our selling methodology to sell direct rather than through sales representatives.

It's twelve years later. I will never forget that day and the subsequent years it took us to pay off the debt. We survived and will continue to go forward.

What I learned:

- During the time when this crisis happened, I'd ask myself, "What can I do today?" And I would do it. I couldn't solve the whole problem at once. I bit off a piece each day. It's the way that we slowly came out of the debt.
- Listen to your gut. I knew that we should have concentrated on our core businesses. Unfortunately, I got outvoted. Now I own the majority of the company so that I can listen to my gut.
- Before you work for a family business, work for another company. I had never worked anywhere else. I think working for another company would have given me some perspective.

Applying the lessons learned to your business:

- Like the previous story, the federal, state, and local government regulations can have a great impact on your business. In this case, they could put your company out of business by eliminating the need for your products and services. If this is the case, you must immediately stop making the products, conserve cash, and determine what products, if any, you can sell to remain in business.
- Make the difficult decisions quickly. Your company's survival may depend on it. Cash conservation is paramount at this time of crisis.

Communicating with your banker and suppliers is critical for survival. It is important to let them know what happened, and that you will get back to them within a specific period of time with a plan. Many times, they will wait for that plan before doing anything legally.

#23

MY PARTNER LOST HIS PASSION
Jeff Fisher
CEO, *Reno Lawn and Landscape*

I'll give you a brief history of my life in the landscape industry. About ten years ago, I stumbled into this business. People ask me if I ever thought when I graduated high school that I would be in this business. The answer was always no. I really didn't even think about anything related to landscaping. This was just the opportunity of the moment. I had just quit another job and my friend owned a landscaping company that needed a general manager. I took the job. Four months later, one of the partners wanted to sell and that's how I began to have partners in the landscaping business. Since 1994, I've had various partners at one time or another in both landscaping and real estate deals.

To be clear, I didn't run off the partners. I bought one partner out after three years, as I merged into the company that I am actually in today. I acquired a new partner through the merger. So, I was a partner again for four years. In 2000, I bought out my latest partner and am the sole owner of the company today. During that time, I also did several real estate deals that involved partners.

In the last partnership, my former partner had been in the business for about nineteen years. I could just see him losing the passion for the business. I woke up one day and realized that either I needed to go away or he needed to go away. On top of that, the job that I really wanted was the job that he had. I knew I could run the operations since I had successfully done it for eight years. I wanted to be the guy going to social events and broadcasting the company name to the public.

A partner is not a partner for life.

So, we sat down in the conference room and I put the plan up on the board. I said either we will be friends at the end of the night or I'll be gone. An hour and a half later, he agreed to the plan. He decided that he was ready to retire.

I had no cash when I got into the business ten years ago. All of my equity got built by using my share of the profits going toward paying for stock. Along the way, I depended on my partners' personal balance sheets to carry us.

So, I had a dilemma when I bought my last partner out. I had no cash. I had to borrow everything, and my personal balance sheet was not as strong as our joint balance sheet.

The biggest thing that happened to me was that through the process of buying my partner out, I also restructured the business and sold off my construction division. I immediately ended up in a lawsuit with the person who bought the construction division. There was some wording in the contract that he used to his advantage and this was at the same time that I was trying to get the SBA loan, borrow money to start up, and visiting my attorney regularly trying to prevent a lawsuit.

I ended up paying him to take the business.

It was January and I had three major debts on my mind. I had to borrow from the Small Business Association to buy out my partner. I had to pay the person who "bought" the construction business, and I had to find the money to start up the season.

The SBA loan didn't even get approved until late in February and in the meantime, I was talking to other bankers to try and borrow money. So there were two months when there was no cash. I was constantly wondering how I was going to make payroll.

It's like my analogy of horseracing: you pick the horse, pick the saddle, but once the race starts, you don't change the saddle.

I ended up finally getting a loan from a local bank for the start-up line of credit for the season. However, for three months I didn't know whether I would have enough for payroll, whether I would own the business and be able to pay for the buyout. And I had lost customers because of the construction deal that basically fell through.

The terror and stress were real. I didn't have a clue whether it would all come together. I finally ended up going to some private investors to fund the business until the bank loans came through. I had to explain the situation and ask. It was incredibly tough, but there was nothing else I could do if I wanted to keep the company open and have it be all mine. They had confidence in my abilities and agreed to loan me the money.

What I learned:

- The SBA loan came through, but not without some problems. The next time I do one I will go to a Tier One bank, which deals with loans all of the time, rather than just a few per year. The process would have been a lot easier.

- If you are going to buy a business, it has to have a structure to operate without the owner. If it doesn't, then it has no value.

- A partner is not a partner for life. This has to be a discussion that you have with potential partners. You have to have a buyout. The interesting thing is that former partners can come back into your life. I'm doing a real estate deal with one now, and my partner who retired at thirty-six is back looking at opportunities with me.

Applying the lessons learned to your business:

- Everything takes longer to accomplish than you think it will. Customer contracts, loans, investments, and agreements are among the things that take days, weeks, or months to complete. Make sure that you have enough cash to take you through until the customer payment, loan, or other cash infusion arrives.
- There's a rule that I live by that seems to work: Whenever someone tells me that it will take X period of time to complete something, I always multiply X by π (3.14). So, if someone tells me it will take a week to complete a contract, I estimate three weeks. It seems to work most of the time. If it is shorter, then I'm ahead.

#24

WE HAD TO GIVE UP CONTROL
Jeff Russell
President, Russell Cellular and Satellite

My challenges and fears have always been people related. My wife and I moved from Arkansas to Missouri on a dream of a better opportunity. We had never been to Missouri before and started there from ground zero.

I did not know a soul in town. However, we just always envisioned that town having a great opportunity. We just picked up one day and drove our little Dodge Omni to Springfield. I grabbed a newspaper and looked for an apartment to rent. I was looking for a job and I actually got into this business by accident. I had seen an ad for a company who wanted someone to sell their phones. I went to work for them. I was the company's only contract labor person. Within ninety days, I found the owner of the company to be terribly unethical. He forced me to go out on my own. That's what I did. We saw an opportunity and started growing it. We've had the business for ten and one-half years.

My wife and I started selling door to door. We wanted an opportunity for more income. We also wanted to control our time. However, I ended up working more than when I had a "job." About six months into the process, I thought that it would be good to have a retail store to service our customers. So, I called my mom and borrowed $1,500 from her. That opened my first store.

It wasn't much of a store. We went to the flea market and bought a used desk and a chair. We put our kitchen table in as a computer hutch, and that's what the phone sat on. That was our first retail office ten years ago. I paid my mom back within thirty days. I opened the second location in our hometown in Arkansas. About one and one-half years later, we opened our third location, which is now our corporate office in Springfield, Missouri.

That is when we sat down with a game plan and starting growing it. That's where the greatest challenge started. However, we succeeded in finding the key to finding good people and today we have forty-four locations. We are Alltel's largest agent in the United States.

It was tough going from being owner and doing everything to being manager and overseeing everything. The first three years of the business, I continued to sell in the field myself and I would manage on the side. I knew I could depend on myself to hit my quota. My quota was what my family needed to live on, so I continued to do that for three to four years into the business even at a point where I had five to six retail stores. I knew I could count on myself regardless of what those retail stores did. So, I juggled two balls for a while until I could afford to back off of my sales and just be a manager.

The only time I stopped was when there was enough cash flow coming in the door to rely on everyone else's sales. Then it got tough. Going from being in the field to managing is hard to do. I felt that one of my strengths was my ability to relate to people. I could take these new people by the hand and teach them what to do. There was nothing in my business my wife and I had not done. As a result, we were very confident when we went to people and told them what to do. We were confident with what we were telling from our experience.

For a long time, I really worked a lot with them. I continued to give them the benefit of the doubt over and over, but eventually I had to come to a point where I had to bring on the right people. We were never going to move forward without bringing the right people on board. That was very hard.

The next big challenge was when I started hiring managers to replace myself as we continued to grow. At every level, I gave up a little bit of what I wanted to achieve with customers.

I felt that no one can represent you as well as you represent yourself.

Letting go is essential for business growth.

That became a big challenge to find people who were like us. They needed to have the attitude, wisdom, and mentality that could do business the way we wanted to do business as well as teach that to our sales representatives.

We actually went and knocked on any doors that we could to find the right people. We did a lot of scouting and I learned from some mistakes. Now our people find the right people. If they don't fit, then our people weed them out themselves. It's actually easier than when I did it by myself.

My biggest challenge was building a "system" from the ground up. "System" is what I use. I consider our company a franchise. We have forty-four stores that are franchises. The system is making sure that everything is done the same across the board.

When it was just me out there selling, I could tweak things or change things quickly and easily. However, when we built it up to ten stores, we couldn't change that quickly. I found that you have to have a playing field. So, we had to build that system from ground zero to make sure it worked for everybody. We had to learn to take somebody brand new who didn't know anything about our business and put them into the system of training, teaching, motivating, and educating them. When they finished the training, they had to be a very knowledgeable salesperson who understands our company, the carrier that we represent, and can represent the customer well.

We had to learn this the hard way. This took a long time to accomplish and was the most frustrating and challenging part. However, I knew to keep going so that the business could continue to grow.

What I learned:

- It is so important to put together your core group of key people. They have to be the right people. Without them, we just could not continue to grow the way we do.
- Money is important in a job, but money is not everything.
- I try to offer a good income to somebody. However, I've learned to offer them things that they are not getting anywhere else: a positive working environment and a successful, motivated team.
- If you get enough good people together in a room and you come to a majority decision, you are going to be

right 99 percent of the time. An individual alone will never achieve that percentage.

Applying the lessons learned to your business:

- Letting go is essential for business growth. Unfortunately, delegation is difficult and must be a learned skill for most entrepreneurs. Without delegation, you will try to do too much and when you are overwhelmed, nothing will get done well.
- Trusting that first manager is critical. Let her make mistakes and learn from them. The more mistakes she makes and the more she learns, the better manager she becomes.
- Once you find a good manager, if you are continuing to grow the business, then start grooming the second manager.
- Managers don't necessarily come from your employees. Many times great employees with specific skills are terrible managers. The skills that make that person great at his job don't translate into the skills that it takes to manage other employees with that skill. If the manager fails, you've lost a great employee. Why? It is the rare person who can admit to his peers that he wasn't a good manager. Most times, they look for another job outside the company.
- Great managers motivate their employees and help achieve the company's goals. The better the

management team, the better the chance that the company will survive crises. In times of crisis, employees rally around and take comfort from good leadership. They know that their ideas will be heard and potentially solve the crisis.

#25

I WASN'T CONFIDENT IN MY ABILITIES
Anonymous

My parents raised me to get good grades and a good job. I followed that track for fifteen years in the world of marketing, sales, and advertising. I went through a lot of conventional job situations. Traditional employment was a problem because I was always ahead of the pack, too impatient with other employees to be part of committees and task forces. Eventually a supervisor came to me and said, "You really do need to start your own company; you have the spirit, the confidence, etc. Rather than piddling around with us, you need to go do your own thing."

In the past, if anyone had mentioned this idea, I was aghast. "Why would anyone do that?" Lo and behold, I got pushed into the situation. Six months after being hired by a new employer, I was forced to leave. My wife and I were days away from receiving our first adopted baby. We were terrified we would lose our baby because of the sudden financial instability. Our only option was to push ahead. We adopted the baby anyway in September of 1991 and started our company thirty days later.

It was scary. I had been pushed out of the nest; I had no choice but to go ahead and do this. I was very fortunate to get a consulting contract almost immediately. That got us off and running. We eventually lost a big client two years into our venture, which put us into a very difficult financial situation because we had no savings.

It was excruciating. I had come from a senior position on the West Coast and wasn't prepared for such a humbling experience. It was very difficult to get clients because I was not known and I had no connections. We lost three-quarters of our income and had to make many lifestyle adjustments that were quite painful.

I dealt with this psychologically by thinking of my venture as glamorous and cutting edge. I was working on my laptop at Starbucks at 9:00 in the morning, collaborating with creative freelancers all over the city. I sipped on a latte, wrote prospecting letters, and envisioned the future. I saw what I was doing as a cool, head-of-the-pack kind of thing. That's how I rationalized my situation during this tough period. My wife's support was also critical, as she picked up extra money working several jobs.

During tough times, I found out that I had to be very careful with whom I discussed our difficulties because even your closest friends can lose respect for you when they learn about your business challenges. They envy you, but they think you're crazy. On a personal, face-to-face level, they are supportive, but they don't send referrals your way. They are even wary about associating with you. It's a torturous thing. Although I needed support during difficult times, I learned to be very careful about opening up to just anyone when I was emotionally upset.

After ten years, I felt I needed to change the game somehow because the grind of not having sufficient money was wearing me down. I was lucky to attract a patient partner, which gave me the courage to go on.

As I reflect on this, there are two levels of fear when going into business. The first involves the struggle with unpredictable cash flow day in and day out. The second is much deeper from a psychological point of view: encountering oneself and asking oneself, "Am I capable of doing this? Why? Am I who I thought I was? If so, then why isn't reality reflecting that? If not, then who am I? And what should I be doing?" Year in and year out, I struggled with those critical issues.

It reminds me of my days in college, where I studied the disparity between what you believe and what's going on around you at the time. For instance, you think you are a talented and hardworking person. There is a supposition that you will have some degree of material success. Yet, you look around and see no evidence of material success.

This is psychological torture.

To cope with this, I realized I had to lose my ego. I studied the premise that none of us is who we think we are. I guess we unconsciously spend a lot of time building up our "stories" of who we are in our head. We have to take a really hard look at our "story." There is a deep philosophical pressure point where you have to drop your pretensions, give up your aspirations, and readjust.

You need to accept the very worst possible scenario and realize that even that won't hurt the real you. You have to go beyond that fear.

Professional challenges drive my self-actualization as a human being.

I still encounter that point every now and then. Acceptance isn't a permanent fix; my ego still flares up and gets hurt when my company doesn't get a client because they think we are too small to merit their business.

To endure the uncertainty, I pray, try to reduce my ego, study philosophy, and seek counsel from certain types of people. Obviously, every time I succeed at work, the pressure lessens somewhat and gives me a sense of relief. But when a client dries up, there is still the sense of "Are we going to be okay?" I know this is my ego talking, grasping for security, yet again.

I do have a couple of people whom I rely upon heavily for reassurance when things are really bad. That has been very helpful. These people have careers that are more traditional and still believe in my ability. They meet me for coffee, reassure me that I have the right stuff, and then send me back into the battle.

I'm still fighting. I have the scars to prove it. But I'm still in the game, thirteen years later.

I'm even optimistic!

What I learned:

- As difficult as it has been, I would never have reached my creative potential if I had stayed in a large company. I grow every day because I get to do everything in my discipline.
- I am very fortunate to do something that I really love...stick my fingers into many different businesses and implement creative solutions. The cross-fertilization of ideas, strategy, and relationships is stimulating. I love that part. I know many people who hate their jobs. In that one respect, I am very lucky.
- Professional challenges may actually drive my self-actualization as a human being. Without the difficulties that go along with being an entrepreneur, I wouldn't have developed such a deep contemplative life and an appreciation for higher realities that transcend conventional notions of success.

Applying the lessons learned to your business:

- Have a team outside the business whom you can trust and rely on. These are people who have your best interests at heart. You may talk with them only once per year. However, you know that the advice that you get is truthful and without hidden agendas. You may not get the same totally truthful, direct opinions from your managers and employees because you as the owner hold the power over them.

- If your employees hate the job they are doing, speak to them about finding something else to generate income. Employees who are not happy are dangerous. Their attitudes harm other employees and your customers sense their unhappiness. Invite the person to go through a "career readjustment program" and find another job (or start his own business).

#26

WE DIDN'T KNOW IF ANYONE WOULD SHOW UP
Rich Schmidt

As a Christian, I feel like God has a plan for each of us. During college, I felt like he was leading me to be a pastor. Then, when I was at seminary, I felt like he was directing me toward church planting (starting new churches and congregations).

I took a class to find out what that would mean. I then went to an assessment center, which looks at people who are called to start new churches. The center evaluates them based on thirteen different criteria, including personality traits, experiences, and other entrepreneurial characteristics. They thought I would be good at church planting, but that I didn't have the personality to go to a brand new community and start from scratch. They recommended that I partner with an existing church that was interested in helping start a new church. That's what I did.

My dad is a pastor in Valparaiso, Indiana, just up the road from where we started. I went on staff with him for nine months to learn the ropes. During that time, we gathered about thirty people who were interested in helping start a church.

My wife and I bought a house in the town where we were going to start the church. We committed ourselves to living and becoming part of the community. We were going for it. There was no turning back. If this didn't work, I couldn't just go back to the parent church and say, "Here I am again. Do you have anything else for me to do and can you pay me?" It was sink or swim time. I felt like Cortez burning his ships.

Our grand opening was in September, 2000. Before the grand opening date, we held sneak preview services in June, July, and August. We all had our roles to play, but we didn't know if anyone was going to show up for the service. We sent out 15,000 direct mail postcards letting people know we were starting a new church and we had sixty to seventy people show for that. A few more came in July, and in August, a few more came. In September, we had 164 people at the service. That was probably the scariest time because if nobody showed up, the church was not going to happen.

I think in the four years that we've been up and running, we've had over one thousand people who have walked through the doors to check us out. The struggle has been communicating clearly to those folks about Christianity and helping them get connected into a church.

We have about 150 people at church services on Sundays. We've had our ups and downs. We'll grow to an average of about 200 people then we'll shrink down to 120. Then we'll grow again. This causes organizational challenges. And I need to find the answers to questions like, "What is limiting our growth? What is keeping us from effectively communicating to people and connecting them into a church?" It is different from a business that is selling a service or a product.

For your company to be successful, you should have managers and employees with varying personality styles.

I have also had a committed team of volunteers who have been around us since we started the church. So, it hasn't just been me with everything riding on my shoulders. From the first day we opened the doors, I was the point person. But there is a team of people helping to make it happen. In some ways that lessened the fear, knowing there were people I could turn to and share the burden. In some ways, it increases the fear because those people are counting on you. I decrease the fear through prayers and guidance from God.

What I learned:

- This experience has taught me that my personality is more toward the introverted side rather than the extroverted side. I've had to learn how to be more outgoing and more of a risk taker.
- I've always been a person who believes that God will come through if you have faith and trust in God. If I am doing what God wants, then things will work. There is nothing like going through an experience that can prove that to you. I've learned that it really is true.

Applying the lessons learned to your business:

- Learn to communicate with and interact with all personality types. It's a lot easier to sell to or work with people who have the same personality style and strengths that you do. However, for your company to be successful, you should have managers and employees with varying personality styles. Different people bring different points of view. These differences are often critical in problem solving and taking care of customers.

- In some cases, the different styles can cause conflict. However, employees need to learn to appreciate the different points of view. They will work more successfully with their fellow employees, managers, and customers.

#27

MY FAITH GOT US THROUGH
Siney Jordan

When I got out of school, I started working for a hair salon. I wasn't happy with the atmosphere in the salon. I worked for another one and still another one. I couldn't find a place where my clientele and I were comfortable. I ended up working out of my house for a while. There had to be a better way.

My husband saw a building that was about five blocks from our house. We found out that it had been empty for about seven years. It was perfect for my shop. My husband and I did the legwork. We wanted to buy it. It was up for sale. A realtor had it, but he wanted about five times what the building was worth. Not an option.

We started working with the neighborhood association where the building was located. We found out that the state had a lien on the building. We called the state and made them an offer. We got our building and I would have my salon. My husband and I did most of the work ourselves, and in December 1997, the shop opened.

Business was good. Clients were happy. As a result, I outgrew the building within a few years. Until then, my clientele had no waiting area or enough space to feel comfortable. We wanted to buy the property around us to expand. That's when the frustration began.

The city kept giving us the runaround. They kept coming up with excuses and things that we had to do. It really felt like they were trying us to see what they could do to us next! It took two years to get the property. And it was a test of faith.

First the zoning. They wanted to keep it residential because it is an area that is up and coming in the city. We had to fight that. After much digging, many prayers, and a lot of tears, we found out that

> *If you want something badly enough, keep going.*

there wasn't enough space to erect a home on the property because of the way that our building is situated. Commercial was the only use for the property. We finally won the zoning.

Then the licensing. Money kept going out the door: $250 here, $1,000 there. At the same time, I was trying to run the business out of a space that we outgrew. We truly believed that the city wanted to harass us to see how much they could put on us to make us quit.

My grandmother owned a restaurant. She lost her building to the city. After the city took her building, I said I would never let this happen to me. I couldn't give up.

There were more meetings, requirements, and hoops that we had to go through. I was so tired. I was pregnant. My son was having problems in school. I thought I was done.

Then my husband wanted to quit. All the time we prayed a lot. We kept asking God if he wanted us to have this building, why were there so many problems? The answer was to keep going. We did. We kept the faith.

Finally! There was nothing else they could "get us for." No more payments before they would approve it. No more hassles. We finally owned it!

I have a nice building now with a good parking lot and landscaping. There is a great waiting area, an office, and a massage room. After all of the stress, the hassles, and everything we went through, I can still say that it has just been a blessing. I will remember the dark days. Even though I wanted to quit many times, my faith and prayers kept me going.

What I learned:

- If you want something badly enough, keep going— even though it seems that it won't happen.
- Prayers and faith in a higher power can get you through.

Applying the lessons learned to your business:

- Local, state, and federal regulations can affect the timing of getting what you want. Make sure you understand the requirements before you look for a business location, expand or remodel your building, or open or move your business. Depending on your type of business, there may be special licenses, parking requirements, or other issues that affect your ability to operate your company. You don't want to be prohibited from starting, or worse, shut down because of not complying with the laws.

#28

I SHOULDN'T HAVE TURNED MY HOBBY INTO A BUSINESS
Beverly Van Horn

We sold our newspaper business for a good sum. I needed to find work because I was only forty-five years old and I knew that we would have income from the sale for only ten years. My husband, twenty years older, thought he would be dead by then, so the ten-year period didn't bother him.

We were in Colorado for the summer and my husband noticed that a Native American gallery was closing. A building was for sale. He thought that I should start my own business because I had always loved Native American jewelry and had managed a gift shop one summer.

I didn't have a business plan and no one ever asked me for one. The bank where I borrowed the money for the business knew me from the newspaper business. They trusted me and made the loan for the building without asking for anything about the new business. I had a note with 16 percent interest without a clue as to what I was doing.

I opened the shop in Colorado. It was going to be open only in the summertime. During the start-up, I decided to sell southwestern clothes too. It seemed like a good addition to the jewelry.

Then we returned to Tucson for the winter. Before I knew it, I was running two part-time businesses in two different locations. While I was in Arizona, I started having jewelry shows in people's homes. I talked about how the jewelry was made and educated the people who attended the shows about how to buy jewelry.

I bought inventory using the money from the newspaper sales. Customers liked what I bought, saying that I had such good taste.

About three years later, I opened a retail store in Arizona. It had to be open all year. So, when I went up to Colorado in the summer, I had to take merchandise with me. It left the Arizona store pretty empty. On top of that, I had to hire someone full time to run it.

I kept bringing merchandise from Tucson to Colorado and back. It was a yo-yo. I wasn't making any money.

Yet, I opened a retail store in Tucson. Why did I do that? I don't know. Again, no plan.

There was never sustainable cash flow. I did not enjoy the business as much as I loved Native American arts and crafts. The clothing was my bread and butter. But because I always owed so much money, I couldn't even enjoy going to market because I was always scared I couldn't pay for the merchandise.

The bank in Colorado had threatened to foreclose on the note and take our house because I was behind on the payments. I was making the interest payments, but hadn't paid off any principal. So, I finally got them to lower the interest rate to 11 percent and to let me have more time. I started paying principal.

My accountant kept telling me I had to get rid of one business or the other. I wanted to get rid of the Colorado business and stay in *Do not start a business* Arizona year round, *without a business plan.* but my husband didn't because he wanted to keep going back up there. Eventually, I discovered he had been abusing the use of credit cards, and could have to file bankruptcy. I divorced him, hoping I could keep my business.

After the divorce, our house did sell in Colorado, so I was able to use my money from that to pay off the bank debt. The good Lord was looking out for me, and I didn't have to go through foreclosure. However, the last straw was when the Arizona business was burglarized. The robbers took all of my jewelry just before the Colorado store would have opened for the summer.

So, I planned to let the bank foreclose on the property if I couldn't sell it that summer. I just wanted to get out of it, come back to Arizona, and get a job with pay.

The following summer I met my new husband. After four more years of summer business in Colorado, I sold the building and moved to Arizona permanently.

For fourteen years I was uptight, nervous, and had stomach problems from just worrying all the time about the money. After I closed the businesses, I found something else to do and my stomach problems are gone.

What I learned:

- Do not start a business without a business plan. Had I done a plan, I would have known more and probably not started.
- Just because you love something as a hobby doesn't mean that it will succeed as a business.
- Retail is very different from other businesses. Make sure you can stand the hours and have money for inventory. Don't buy what you like. Buy what will sell.

Applying the lessons learned to your business:

- As a business owner, you have to work on your business as well as in your business. Planning and executing that plan are critical to your business survival. You need a team of outsiders to help you. A board of directors or an advisory board will help keep you focused. When you have to report the positive and the negative to the board, you keep up-to-date and are required to focus on the goals and objectives that the group sets for the business. You will also rely on the team for advice when issues arise. This increases your chances of business - success.

#29

I DIDN'T HAVE ANY SUPPORT
Christine Kloser
CEO, New Entrepreneurs, Inc.

As I grew up, I didn't fit into the expected norm. I knew that going to college, doing interviews, and getting a job—the whole nine to five routine—was not for me. I just couldn't do it. I knew I didn't want to live a traditional lifestyle, but didn't have any exposure or knowledge that an entrepreneurial life was an option for me. Becoming an entrepreneur took me by surprise.

I started my first business in 1991 doing something I had always done throughout my life...exercise. I effortlessly started a home-based personal training business with one client who lived right on my street. It was really fun getting paid for something I liked to do and the best part was she liked it too and spread the word to her friends. Before I knew it, I had lots of clients and a booming business. I soon discovered yoga and decided to open a private personal training gym and yoga studio. Later I took over an existing yoga business in a larger studio.

The biggest challenge was I didn't know any other entrepreneurs. All my friends had jobs with benefits and couldn't relate to my entrepreneurial dedication. They didn't get me and couldn't understand why I was working so hard. At times, I ended up working twelve-hour days, sometimes seven days a week. There were weeks I taught nearly thirty hours of yoga classes.

There had to be a support system available to over-worked entrepreneurs like me. I knew I needed to find a group like this or I wasn't going to be in business much longer. But where could I find them? I searched Los Angeles looking for these women and found a few professional organizations. But to me, they were missing the heart of supporting and helping each other. It felt like the primary purpose of these groups was to exchange business cards and refer business to each other. That wasn't what I was looking for. I wanted to find a group of women who supported my business, and kept me inspired and motivated to keep going.

At this point, in 2000, I had three years of volunteer experience leading women's groups for non-business purposes. So, I decided to combine my leadership ability with my desire for a like-minded business community and started my own group. On the first Thursday of each month, I began to bring together a few of my own friends and share my ideas with them. Here's the funny part. None of the friends who came to my first meeting in April 2000 had their own businesses; they just wanted to come out for Chinese food.

I held my vision strong, and told them I wanted us to meet each month and talk over dinner about entrepreneurialism. I envisioned the five or ten of us would ask questions and help each other out. No matter what, I kept holding

If you want to be successful, you have to get a handle on the numbers.

meetings the first Thursday of every month. Four years later, without any marketing or advertising, there are more than five hundred members and four chapters of my women's organization called the Network for Empowering Women Entrepreneurs (most commonly known as NEW Entrepreneurs, or simply NEW). Now, I get to have dinner on the first Thursday of the month with seventy-five incredible like-minded, successful, and spirited entrepreneurs.

However, here was the tough part. While NEW was growing, my yoga studio was operating at a $3,000/month loss. I was carrying about $10,000 a month of overhead to keep the doors open, not including a salary for myself and my husband, who helped me run it. We generated about $7,000 a month gross income.

Living in that $3,000 deficit every month got to the point where I felt that someone had to take over the lease or we would be locking the doors and filing for bankruptcy.

Thankfully, in October 2002, we found buyers who were willing to give us six figures for the business. We negotiated. We were ready to close the deal when they found out something I didn't know when I took over the business. It turned out the business did not have the proper certificate of use to have a yoga studio at that location. We couldn't get one because we didn't have enough parking to fulfill the city's requirements. After seven months of negotiations, all the while losing $3,000 per month, we couldn't come to a mutual agreement with the buyers and they didn't purchase the business. I was crushed and at the end of my rope.

One half of my life was more stressful than you can imagine and the other half of my life I saw a business I loved grow and grow and grow. It was an interesting, exciting, and devastating year.

Thankfully, someone took over the lease one day before we were ready to lock the doors and begin the process of filing for bankruptcy. I'm grateful the yoga studio is only a memory. Owning that business was, by far, the most challenging time of my life. Sometimes I wonder how my husband and I made it through. Thank goodness, we had each other; I don't think I could have made it through the devastation alone.

When I think back on that time, it is almost impossible to believe it was only one year ago. Now, my only business is NEW, the one I love. It continues to grow and expand in unexpected and wonderful ways. Sometimes it's so good, I have to pinch myself to believe it's real. I'm making the most money I've ever made doing something I love that doesn't feel like work at all. The best part is I have an enormous community of like-minded women who support me to be my best in my personal, business, spiritual, and financial life. And being of service to help them have the same in their life is the greatest blessing of all.

What I learned:

- Do what you love. If you're going to be successful in business and in life, you've got to be passionate about what you do.
- Research everything you can about the business you want to get into.
- Learn the numbers part of the business. That's what I didn't do when I made the decision to move into the studio that nearly sank me. I was a little too optimistic. If you are going to be successful in business, you have to get a handle on the numbers.
- Surround yourself with people who have a "you can" attitude rather than a "you can't" attitude. It's your responsibility to seek out and find like-minded people who are going to lift you up and believe in you. Most of the population lives in "I can't" fear, doubt, and worry. Spend time with people who live in possibility, faith, abundance, and love.

- Just because you failed at something doesn't mean you are a failure as a human being. It simply means you failed at something you tried to do. Look for the lessons from the failure and use them to guide you in a new and more powerful direction.

Applying the lessons learned to your business:

- Understanding the financial side of your business is critical. Monthly financial statements are necessary to spot minor issues before they become major crises.
- You cannot abdicate the reading of financial statements to anyone else in your company. If it is your business, you are ultimately responsible for the profits and losses. Get help if you don't understand how to read them. Learn enough to question the statements that you receive. Asking questions of your bookkeeper, accountant, and others involved with the financial end of your business is perfectly acceptable.
- Demand that you get the financial information by the 15th of each month. This is the best way to keep on top of what is going on with your business.

#30

A COMPETITOR POACHED MY EMPLOYEES
Tom Powell
President and Founder, IntoHomes, LLC

I grew up poor in one of the richest areas of Reno, Nevada. I started my first business at thirteen, partly because it added to my sister's meager salary that we were living on, and partly because I loved having my business—MACOW—Millions Are Coming Our Way. I had talked the local bank manager into letting me open a checking account, and I figured out that I could make more money hiring my friends to do the work and then paying them a fair wage. This simplistic version of entrepreneurship, while a necessity, became a passion that I now live, eat, and breathe every day.

I was managing a retail store by the time I was sixteen, and it helped pay my way through college in the San Francisco area. My managerial skills caught the attention of a friend who worked for a major bank. Before I knew it, I was recruited and soon became the youngest vice president in the bank's 140-year history. There I learned about commercial lending and I knew it was a field in which I had a natural, unique ability.

Having lived in the city for several years, I moved back to Reno to establish myself in business. I started a couple of small companies, none of which succeeded. No matter what, I kept coming back to lending. Even though I had been a commercial lender, I quickly transitioned into residential lending. Reno was small, and it was easy to get into the mortgage business since the barrier to entry was so low. I made a lot of money, and I made it fast. Becoming a success, however, was another story.

In 1992 and 1993, there was a huge housing boom. People wanted mortgages and I supplied them. Business was great. In 1994, though, the market started to change and then began a steep dive as interest rates moved up. Having realized early on that "it's not the loan, it's the experience," I stayed focused and gave my clients the most amazing service they had ever received in getting a home loan.

It paid off. In 1995, during one of the worst years in the mortgage industry, I had the opportunity to buy a piece of the mortgage company where I worked. I jumped at the chance, and my company became a net branch (similar to a franchise) of the Hammond Company. While mass chaos reigned and other companies were going out of business, 1995 turned out to be one of the biggest growth years for me.

I had a great team and we were centered in the marketplace. We stayed very, very focused on our key message, which was that we "put people into homes." This became our jingle in radio advertising and our message in print advertising. Eventually, it became our name. We also stayed focused on the fact that we were different from others; we truly cared about each client and their circumstances. We knew that if we provided excellent service, we would have them for life, not just for a transaction.

During the next four years, we had our share of frustrations as our affiliated companies went through several changes. One retired. Another decided he didn't want to be in the mortgage business and got out. The third ran into financial trouble and headed into bankruptcy nearly taking us with them. Yet, we stayed on message of "putting people into homes," and "it's not the loan, it's the experience," and rode out each change and wave.

Each change brought a new operating name, which was expensive and confusing to clients. Finally, I decided to take a leap and form my own company. IntoHomes, LLC was formed on June 26, 1999. I made sure everyone in northern Nevada knew about my company. I spent an astronomical amount on advertising, website design, and mailings. We were successful. We were getting noticed. I wanted to expand the company exponentially. And yet, I was creating a huge debt load to make it all happen.

Three years ago, I decided to bring in new investors. The agreements were made and the attorneys had everything ready to be signed. We were about to pull the trigger when a major bank came to town with a huge checkbook and began recruiting my top producers. The industry had never seen a boom like this before; it was much like the dot-com frenzy in the nineties. They made ludicrous offers to my people, offers they simply couldn't refuse and which I couldn't match.

One by one, my team members started bailing out. In a very short period of time, I went from offering a quality, profitable company to my investors to having that valuable asset evaporate very quickly. I had a very difficult meeting with the investors and told them what was happening. Their answer was very reassuring. They said, "We're investing in you and we trust you. It's okay if we need to shrink and rebuild."

I went back to the remaining staff and said, "Guys, if we need to go down to five people, we will rebuild from the people who want to be here and remain a part of this team." Our lowest point was thirteen team members, down from around thirty.

We made it through. It has been a hard two years since our partnership agreement became final; during that time, we grew back up to twenty-eight and have now settled at eighteen, with the goal to slowly grow back to around twenty-five. Overall, focus kept us pushing forward, and now that every-

If you don't love what you're doing, then you should be doing something else!

thing has settled, 2004 is turning out to be a great year. The investors are happy with the returns, and we are happy with the quality of life we now have. I have found that while change can be difficult, it always works out for the best.

What I learned:

- You have to be focused, tenacious, and confident to be successful. Good things will happen. Bad things will happen. Keep focused on your goals. For me, I kept our team focused on "putting people into homes" and "it's not the loan, it's the experience." If you don't love what you're doing, then you should be doing something else!

- As a president and owner who works within the business, my behavior and attitude determine the office atmosphere. It is up to me to maintain a positive, mentoring attitude as much as possible. When I'm positive and happy, so is my team. When I'm frustrated and upset, the tension builds and it's detrimental to the entire office.

Applying the lessons learned to your business:

- Focus is critical. Keep implementing your business plan with an eye on external forces, i.e., the economy or your competition. If your managers and employees get worried about the external forces, as the owner, it is your responsibility to reinforce the positive. Listen to their concerns. However, if the company is doing well, despite the negative external forces, point that out, and make sure everyone continues doing what is making the company - successful.

- It is your responsibility to keep an eye on that negative (or positive) external force and be prepared to act quickly if those forces start affecting your business.

#31

OUR ADVISORS BETRAYED US
Julia Barredo Willhite
Owner, Bilingual Integrated Services

I was born in Cuba and came to the United States when I was eight. This was the land of opportunity if you worked hard. I got my education and became a Spanish teacher. My husband's job relocated him to Memphis, Tennessee, so I started teaching there.

One day my husband said, "I've got this idea for a business. Let's explore it. I want you to be the owner because it would make us more eligible for financing and breaks, etc."

We did extensive research, got our costs in line, incorporated, and opened Our Autumn Years. This was an adult day care where you could take grandma during the day. You could bring Alzheimer patients. You could bring dementia patients. Right before we had to close, we were looking at a contract with the city for them to send us all their rehab patients.

That was the start of the nightmare. We applied for a Small Business Administration (SBA) loan. Of course, with an SBA loan you have to have everything ready before they give you the money. My husband's and my projections were better than on target. We came in below cost projections.

The building was ready. Then, ten days before we were supposed to close on our loan, we couldn't get in touch with our attorney. We constantly called his office. All they would say was that he wasn't there.

We went to the closing without our attorney. Our banker said, "I've got good news and I've got bad news." The loan did come through, but it didn't come through for the amount that we asked for. He quoted us a sum that was $75,000 less than what we had asked for.

My husband looked him in the eye and said, "You've signed our death warrant. That was our bridge money."

Now we had to close the business. We had a moral and ethical obligation to stay open through the end of the month. We sold our vehicles. We sold our house. We did what we had to do to make sure that our employees got paid through the end of that month that we closed. We paid their insurance through the end and gave them good letters of recommendation.

> *When you are starting a business, do as much as you possibly can yourself.*

The ironic part is that $75,000 would have allowed us to operate while we negotiated the contract with the city of Memphis. We would have been guaranteed fifteen to thirty clients per day. But we couldn't do the contract because we didn't have the funds to stay open.

At this point, I had a six-year-old child and my income as a teacher couldn't support a whole lot of people. We had to declare business bankruptcy and we had to declare personal bankruptcy because all those personal guarantees that we made came rushing in.

We found out later that we were one of four different businesses that our former attorney and banker took advantage of. The loan was approved for the original amount. The banker and the attorney took the $75,000 for themselves and put us in bankruptcy.

Now this is year eight past the business and year seven past the personal bankruptcy. We have recovered like the phoenix rising from the ashes. Even with the bankruptcy, if we could do our own financing or find a reasonable investor, we would do it again in a New York minute.

What I learned:

- I placed too much trust in my attorney and my banker. I thought that they were on my side, but it turned out that they weren't.
- Look for alternative methods of financing. For example, one of the areas they turned us off to was a fund available to women entrepreneurs. I would jump into that area the next time because I was the president and CEO.

- I would do more myself in the beginning. We didn't do our own marketing and advertising, even though I had worked for an advertising agency in New York. Nobody knew my business as well as I did at that point and I could have produced everything.
- Explore alternative methods. Don't immediately trust without exploration. We handed things off to people that we shouldn't have.
- The experience made our marriage stronger.

Applying the lessons learned to your business:

- When you are starting a business, do as much as you possibly can yourself. Cash conservation is the rule. If the project must take your time or your money, let it take your time. You can trust that it will get done on time with minimum monetary expense.
- There are many sources of funding for start-up, new, and established businesses. Your banker, accountant, and other financial advisors can help you locate non-traditional sources. Explore all of them. Determine what you are willing to use as collateral for the funding and what amount of control (if appropriate) you are willing to give up for the funding. Whomever you get funding from, make sure that source helps the business with something other than funding. You'll likely need help or advisors in your business operations. The funder

should be able to help or suggest someone who can. It is in their best interest to do this. However, many don't unless asked.

And a P.S.

There was some humor despite all of the stress while we were going through the bankruptcies. Once you get on the bankruptcy court rolls, you have all sorts of credit companies calling offering to fix your credit for you. One young man had seen me on the bankruptcy list and called me. He said, "I'm going to tell you that I can save you pennies on the dollar. I can work with you and you won't have to file bankruptcy."

I said, "Oh man, that is awesome."

He replied, "How much do you owe?"

I said, "By the time you throw everything in, I think it is $378,000."

Silence on the telephone.

Finally, he says, "That is over a quarter of a million dollars."

"Yes, sir."

His reply, "Oh honey, go ahead and file bankruptcy—nobody can help you!"

#32

EMOTION GOT IN THE WAY
Donna Fox
President, By Special Arrangements, Inc.

Financial crises have always made me panic. My companies have experienced some major financial losses, which I'm okay with, but it's times when you only have four dollars in your checking account that cause panic. You just have to figure it out. The last time I ran to the bank and got a cash advance through my credit card until I could sell some assets. Lesson learned: remember to pay yourself!

Probably the hardest part about being an entrepreneur is keeping all the balls in the air; all the plates spinning at one time. I can't tell you how many times I've forgotten to pay my personal bills because my business bills are the ones I think of first. I run a number of companies, so keeping all the different hats in order is probably the biggest challenge that I face.

After I got out of law school, I had nothing but a whole lot of debt. I first sold my soul in a big law firm for a few years. I went into law with the ideological sense of helping people. I quickly realized that it didn't work that way, even though I tried many different areas of law.

I was thinking about settling down in some public interest law so at least I would feel good about what I was doing. I was shocked to find out it didn't pay well. The jobs that I found offered $24,000 per year. I was getting a divorce and I knew I couldn't support myself on that.

I was disillusioned. I wasn't helping anyone and I realized that I wasn't getting anywhere myself. I reached the point where I had to get out of that.

I went into business. I wanted to be on my own and reap the fruits of my labor. The first business was a vending business. I just wanted to see how the vending business worked. Not a good fit. We sold it and broke even.

The second business was real estate. The third was a teleconferencing company where we held classes for entrepreneurs. The fourth was a real estate Internet site. We bought undervalued assets, whether in real estate or business.

While we were creating the curriculum for our Automatic Income through Systems seminar, we realized that every real mistake we made was because we deviated from the system we set up for the *If a deal sounds too good to be true, it probably is.* businesses. These were things like letting relationships get in the way of business, doing deals without getting the contract signed, or relying on reputation of an investor rather than doing the necessary due diligence. We knew better. However, we were being emotional, rather than logical.

Relying on friendships rather than doing a system is really the mistake. In a nutshell, we realized to avoid the fears and hardships, you must figure out what your system is going to be for that business. Don't deviate from it unless there is a business reason; not a situational reason and definitely not an emotional reason to do so. Improve the system instead of deviating from the system.

Almost every time we messed up, we were really eager for the deal—there was hunger. That is an emotional place. It took us a long time and tens of thousands of dollars to realize that the deal of a lifetime comes around every couple of months.

What I learned:

- Remember to pay yourself.
- Don't get emotional. If I want a deal too badly, it usually isn't a good deal.
- It's the system that counts. Follow the system and it will be okay.
- The "deal of a lifetime" comes around every couple of months.

Applying the lessons learned to your business:

- If a deal sounds too good to be true, it probably is. Many times, you will want a sale so badly that you may give away too much in the negotiations. On the other hand, you may need financing so badly that you'll give up too much. This could cause major problems later.

- If you are emotional about an employee, an event, or a customer, it is very difficult to think logically about that person or event. Logic, rather than emotions, is required to deal with the situation. Speak with someone who can provide perspective so that you can get rid of the emotion and use logic to determine the right outcome.

#33

WE OPENED AT THE WORST TIME
Christopher Pollock

I have been in the hotel business most of my life. We were planning to open a new hotel in Florida and we were six months late in opening. In Florida, the season is January through May. We missed it. In addition, the cost was $2 million more than we expected. We had to get open, so we opened in June, 2001. Not a good time for the tourist business in Florida.

Everything was on top of us. We opened in the slower season. The economy had started to slide. We were trying to maintain a four-star rating. The hotel was 35 percent occupied on the morning of September 11, 2001.

September is traditionally the slowest time of year and we had a couple of small groups in the house when we all heard about the terror attacks. I thought to myself, not again. I had been running a hotel in the Virgin Islands when the United States invaded Kuwait.

Having experienced this before, my personal stress was high, but I knew what I had to do. I immediately went into action. We contacted all the guests we could to let them know what happened and told them to check with their airline. Within a short amount of time, everybody realized that the whole airport system was shut down.

I decided that if there were guests there who couldn't leave, then the hotel wasn't going to charge them. We tried to help people get home. In one case, I arranged for a rental car, which a group used to drive to the Midwest.

I knew business was going to drop dramatically and I had to do something. Our company called a meeting, and nine days after 9/11, we all flew to Cleveland to look at how we could cut costs drastically. Unfortunately, being a new hotel was a lot more difficult because you open with certain expectations.

We had sessions so employees could come and ask what was going to happen. As we started formulating our cost-reduction program, we had to be very honest. The unfortunate part was a lot of employees hadn't been with the hotel long enough that they could collect any unemployment.

We tried to rotate and reduce hours as much as we could, but at some point, we had to actually lay some people off. We ended up having to cut services and hours of the lounge, the restaurant, and the concierge's lounge. I ended up having to lay off between 20 and 25 percent of our staff, which was not fun to do. That was the hardest part of the whole deal.

Somehow, we got through September. We knew that if we could make it to October we would be in better shape. The largest boat show in the world comes in October and visitors to the show needed hotel rooms. We were all very *Look at the future in addition to handling the immediate.* concerned because the room bookings were down. Not as many people were going to come. In the end, it turned out to be a pretty decent week for us. That gave us all a sigh of relief and a little bit of hope.

November slowed down again. We had a fairly decent Christmas. We managed to make it through. We kept it flexible, we got the employees to understand that if the customer needs something and it is not available, get it yourself or make the effort. The majority of the staff did understand what was going on. There was quite a bit of "We don't want anyone laid off, so I'll take a couple of days off and let someone else work." That made me feel good.

About a year later, I got the opportunity to lead a hotel association. After I opened the hotel in June 2001, and went through 9/11, I decided that the hotel business was something I didn't want to do anymore. The hotel is still open and doing well.

What I learned:

- Take action immediately. Managers and I met the afternoon of 9/11 and started planning.
- Look at the future in addition to handling the immediate. We reacted to the customers immediately, but put plans in place for the following week and the following months.

Applying the lessons learned to your business:

- Recognize when emergency plans must be implemented and do it. The hard decisions will save your business.
- Once you get through an emergency, then you'll recognize it the next time it happens, if it happens. You will be better equipped to handle the situation fast and have the confidence to get through it.

#34

DUE DILIGENCE WASN'T ENOUGH
Larry Duckworth

I am a serial entrepreneur. I've spent my life looking for hidden value in technology businesses that can be brought forward to great shareholder value. I find the right team to help me build them. Then I exit at good multiples and good returns to shareholders...many times to our competition because we've become too much of a threat.

My latest business, a learning solutions company, has provided me with the greatest challenge yet. I first learned about the company while I was actively performing M&A and Executive Consulting for EGL Holdings and GE Equity, after selling my workforce management software company for an excellent multiple. EGL had been contracted by the learning company to help with partnering, with which I assisted, and the company later approached me to be CEO.

I turned down the initial offers. They kept upping the incentives because they knew of my track record. They knew I had been successful and I *hate* to lose. Finally, they made an offer that I couldn't refuse. The risk-reward ratio was right. I remembered the statement that "In the end, it is the risks we never took that we regret most."

I did my normal due diligence, although somewhat limited by two major consulting jobs and deadlines. I talked to the company's major customer who represented 80 percent of the company's revenues. This was an obvious risk that had to be evaluated! However, it seemed they were happy with the company and indicated that they were going to continue using the company to provide online training for their 50,000+ employees.

I talked to the employees and looked at the software. It seemed solid. An independent expert's analysis had been positive, with some needed, achievable improvements noted. Other smaller customers were happy with it. I felt this was an opportunity for me to make my next mark and win again, especially for some local investors.

I later realized that I didn't do enough due diligence. Four months after I agreed to join the company, the software crashed at the major account. And it crashed hard. How did this happen? Because of a good thing. Based on introducing two major new learning programs, tens of thousands of new user employees logged on, signed up for, and started taking a new class that we promoted. It brought the system to its knees.

When we examined the software from the inside out, under the smooth-looking exterior, we discovered the code couldn't be scaled. That caused the crash. The seemingly good growth problems that were bubbling under the surface had finally boiled to the top with this latest major increase in employees taking the new class. The data model would have to be changed along with much of the 800,000 lines of logic coding.

There are always things you can't see until you are in the trenches.

On top of the software issues, our customer, who was supposedly happy according to my due diligence, issued a long-planned, it turned out, request for proposals/information to locate other possible vendors who could supply what we supplied to them. It was obvious that our major customer was in danger of being lost. Suddenly we would be a small business now competing against IBM, Siebold, SAP, and other *Fortune* 500 companies for our survival.

While the problems started before my "watch," I accepted the challenge and I am leading the company. My usual response when we find issues that could affect a customer, besides fixing the problem, is to go to the customer, take the heat, and resolve the problem. I didn't do it this time. Why? Because I was new and didn't have the long-term relationship with the customer that our account team did. After running this by the customer, they said not to go and not to push it. I listened to them rather than my gut. I wish I had trusted my instincts and been proactive.

Now we are in the process of even greater damage control and are fighting for our existence. Can a small company beat the *Fortune* 500? Can David beat Goliath? I think so.

We totally rewrote the solution in two and a half months. It was a Herculean effort that should have taken six months. It now works, there is no spaghetti code in it, and the data model is powerful and scalable. We also were proud of how well the solution had been adapted to the customer. We supplied our cheerleaders in our major customer's company with ammunition for the RFP. They have over two hundred detailed key success criteria, which we supply to use in the RFP. Also, we made sure to meet our deliverables and give them a feeling of commitment and dependability. After all, the vendor selection may affect the continuity of careers.

Fortunately, our largest customer didn't turn off the revenue switch during this rewrite of the software. There still is a possibility that they could turn to another vendor and drop our company.

I searched around for other markets that needed our platform and programs on a "mission critical" basis. We won several customers. The focus on sales and finding and winning new customers is forefront in everyone's minds...including the software programmers. The options were reissued at better strike prices and vesting set to a stretch but achievable revenues amount. New options were also issued and bonuses paid.

Every week we win new, happy customers. Every week we become more of a competitive threat. Every week we lessen dependence on a large customer, who will also be forever important to us no matter the size we get. We never forget our friends.

Will we survive? I don't know. However, the odds are at least fifty-fifty. And as an entrepreneur, I hate to lose.

What I learned:

- As the leader, I think the stress is good. It keeps us on our toes. It keeps everyone focused, the subconscious mind working, and the spirit of the people fighting in the same direction. We definitely aren't complacent. We definitely aren't bored. Fear can be a very good thing.
- I should always listen to my gut.

- I put the crises in perspective. When someone is yelling at me or someone does something really stupid that costs a lot of money or a contract, I remember the times in the military under even greater stress. Nothing in business has been as bad as a situation where your life and limb are at stake. That's stress.

- Even though I thought that I performed with due diligence and asked the right questions, there are always things that you can't see until you are in the trenches. You've got to be good enough to handle the crises as they arise. Ice water in the veins and coolness under fire (a genetic trait I have) is essential to clear-headed thinking and keeping the team focused, optimistic, and performing.

- And it is good to remember what Patton reputedly said, "The secret to winning is not to lose!"

Applying the lessons learned to your business:

- Always get input from your managers and employees. If they have worked with customers in the past, they have a sense of how to work with those customers. However, you have to make the final decision and have responsibility for that decision. Do your research of the situation. Think about the intended and unintended consequences of your actions. After the research, if your gut is telling you to do something that is different from what the managers recommend, then go with your gut instinct.

- If one customer has most of your business, fear of loss of that customer can cause you to acquiesce to the customers' demands even when those demands create an unprofitable situation for you. Do not fear saying "no" to an unprofitable demand. If you say yes, that unprofitable demand could put you out of business.

#35

I LET MY GREED OVERRIDE MY COMMON SENSE
Anonymous

Here is the story that is every entrepreneur's nightmare. I was in an airport reading through magazines. An article caught my attention. It said something like "Earn $1 million or $2 million." It was in a respected business magazine. Normally I never look at those things, but for some reason I tore this one out. When I got home, I made the phone call.

The business was about Comprehensive Outpatient Rehabilitation Facilities or CORFs. The person on the telephone claimed to grow up in the same location I was in. I felt a little more comfortable and asked more about what the business was about.

The person explained CORFs and said that the geographic area that I was in would handle three locations. And I could set one up a few hours from my location. He further explained that their company knew how to get through all of the red tape to get them set up. And, by the way, they are very profitable.

I would have a doctor who would become our medical director. This person wouldn't work for me on a full-time basis, but he would review the charts, etc.

We talked about an hour or so and it sounded interesting. He said that if I was interested, I could come to Phoenix to go through a whole day orientation. And, if I was still interested after the orientation, I could go to the next step.

The daughter of my assistant at the time was working in rehabilitation in another state. I called her and told her about this deal. I asked her what she thought. She made me believe that what they were saying made some reasonable sense. The place that she was working did blood transfusions for people at their homes. Even though it was a small building, the company grossed several million dollars. That peaked my interest even more. There was money to be made.

I asked her to fly with me to Phoenix. She agreed, so I paid for her to go with me to listen to this deal. I felt she would know the technical side and I could understand the business side.

The orientation lasted about eight hours. There were about forty interested people. Several people from the company talked with us. They talked about some of the technical side, but talked mostly about the profit/loss side of the business. And it just looked great. On the way back to the airport, I said to her, "Does this seem like it could be a scam?" I should have listened to my gut.

I had met another man down there by the name of Charlie (name changed) who agreed to stay in contact with me. We started the due diligence together. We did this for about a three-week period. There were some red flags there, but we kept getting past the red flags. Of course, we shouldn't have, but we did. The biggest one was they would not give us any people's names, even though they said they had three hundred other CORFs set up throughout the United States. That was private information.

They did give us people we could talk to. There were five people in four different locations. I talked with two in Dallas and flew down to look at their facility. I met with them for about five or six hours and went over every single bit of financial information that CORF had given me. They said that their facility was going great. Everything you see in there surpassed what they've given us and they were looking to open a third one. They seemed like nice successful business guys. So, I talked to everyone else and all of them said the same thing.

At one point through all this, I started to believe that this wasn't a scam. I just had to prove what they were saying made sense. You paid $165,000 for them to set you up on one facility. They came in and helped you find the facility, did the lease with you, and it was almost like a franchise. They helped you get the license and get through all the red tape. If you got a second one, you pay only half of that and the other half at eighteen months.

One would never be good enough for me. I decided I had to get two in my primary location and was going to get a third, then a fourth after that. I had visions of multiple centers in multiple locations across the United States. I started the search for private placement money and to bring other investors in.

In June 2002, I wrote them a check for $250,000 and went to owner's orientation in Phoenix. We spent two days there. I was so excited that I was coming out of my skin during the orientation. I couldn't wait to get going on this.

I came back waiting for our person who was supposed to come help us set everything up. Two or three weeks went by and I didn't hear from this person. In the meantime, I was working diligently on putting a private place-

It does you no good to sit and cry over spilled milk.

ment memorandum together to bring investors in. I went to a friend who was running an engineering firm and convinced him to move so that he could run the facilities. He agreed to do it for a piece of the profit.

Around July 22, 2002, I got an unsolicited email. Someone from the company made a mistake and emailed all three hundred CORFs. She didn't blind copy the emails, so I finally got everyone's addresses. So all of sudden everybody that got the email also got everyone else's email addresses. At this point, I still didn't know anything. The email didn't bother me and I just dismissed it.

The next day I got a phone call from the lady who was supposed to come help set up the medical group for me. She said, "By the way, there is another CORF that is set up in your location right now. They are struggling, so I don't think they can support more than one CORF there."

I just sat there going, "What?!" I had been promised a CORF. However, nothing has been put in writing from these people because we were licensees. I asked her what she was talking about. I was supposed to have X, Y, and Z. She offered to put me in another location. My big thing was to build multiple ones so you had efficiencies. You could have one medical director in charge of three of these things and so on.

That opened up the floodgates. At this point, I said, "This is obviously not what I've agreed to. You've told me completely different things."

I went back to those emails and started emailing. By the end of that evening, I had talked with three or four more people who told me absolute horror stories. These businesses were not producing anywhere near the revenue that they were claiming. I talked to one guy who was very close to my location who asked me to take his since he had put $500,000 in it and was close to bankruptcy.

So, I talked to a lawyer. I'm trying to figure out how to save the $250,000 that they have of mine.

First, I have a very supportive wife. As I was talking about what-ifs, my wife looked at me and said, "Are these the kinds of people you want to be in business with?" I realized she was exactly right. I'd had such a clouded thought process going on.

I sent them a demand letter to get my money back. Of course, I haven't gotten it. My friend Charlie had the same thing happen to him, except he only put in $165,000 rather than my $250,000. The lawsuit involved almost forty people.

The company has gone bankrupt and I think my chance of getting any money back is about zero.

What I learned:

- It has been an unbelievable time. I am a big proponent of getting a lot of people's advice and I have done that my entire career. I talked to a lot of different people. Part of the problem with what happened was that I got very enthusiastic, too enthusiastic, and I started convincing whomever I was talking to that it was a good deal.

- I missed it because of greed. I got so excited about making so much money that I started to make excuses for them on why this or that didn't make sense. I think I was the biggest part of missing it. I couldn't wait to open up enough of these and I thought I had hit the big time. It clouded all my judgment.

- The biggest red flag was not being able to talk with others. The four people that they gave us were shills who were paid by them.

- From my standpoint, I had never been ripped off in my life in previous companies. There were some companies who didn't pay their bills, but those were minor incidents. I had never dealt with people that were dishonest like that and so good at doing it.

- I've matured as a businessman. I'm doing more due diligence and taking more time. If it is a great opportunity, it will be there in the future for me. If I had taken another month, it would have saved me $250,000.

- You can sit and cry over the spilled milk, but it does you no good. I've always felt that way. It would bother me more at certain times, but other than that, you just keep moving because there is nothing you can do about it.

Applying the lessons learned to your business:

- When your desire for money is the sole reason for starting a business, then it is likely to fail. Why? Because you become emotional about decisions rather than logical. Step back and look at the opportunity rationally. If it appears too good to be true, it probably is. However, if you can't see that because emotions are blinding you, then you may spend a lot of money with no return.

- Look very hard when evaluating business opportunities. Rather than just talking with the business seller, find someone in an allied business that you can talk with. Get another perspective on the business. Owners in noncompeting areas are very likely to speak with you truthfully if you tell them you are thinking about purchasing a business. Ascertain whether this is a type of business you want to be involved with from a logical, rather than an emotional, viewpoint.

#36

A KEY EMPLOYEE LEFT
Ryan Allis
CEO, Broadwick Corporation

I worked for a company in Florida that sold nutraceutical products. We had developed a large subscriber list of around 60,000 people. When we sent out our newsletters each month, we had to tie up a computer for about twenty-four hours to send it out. There had to be a better way.

Then, I moved to Chapel Hill to go to college. While there, I met a person who had developed the base of the software that had the features that I needed. We decided to joint venture. I would market that software. Eventually in early 2003, we decided to form a third company that would develop, market, and commercialize the software. That's how Broadwick Corporation was started.

There were many, many issues. First was the equity structure of the new company. We had two major partners. However, four or five other people were going to work with us or invest money. We had negotiations with one person and then brought the results to the second person. Then to the third, fourth, etc. The back and forth yo-yo took about two months to get it all straightened out.

> *Very rarely does everything come together before you start. Just start.*

We didn't take a salary. We brought on our first employee in September 2003, and that was the most terrifying part. We didn't know whether that person would have a job in thirty days. We felt an obligation to that person who was working for us, but we didn't know whether we could keep him. It turned out that we could.

I would say that the most stressful parts were in the fall and early winter when we didn't really know if we were going to make it as a company. We didn't know if we would get enough customers to cover our debt and to cover our payroll. It was worse when we hired a developer in February. Would we be able to keep him on?

Since we are still small, each employee that we've hired is critical to our success. Our first employee left after six months to go to graduate school. We had to find a good replacement and we totally underestimated the time that it would take to find someone good. We thought that we would find someone in a couple of weeks. It took much longer.

We interviewed about twenty people and finally settled on one about a week before he was about to leave. On her first day of training, she just didn't come in. We worked hard to decide on someone who was going to be crucial to our business. Then that person decides it's not for them. We were so frustrated that we had to start all over. So, we did what we had to do.

In the meantime, we had to take care of all of the customers and support for our rapidly growing company. Everyone put in long hours to take up the slack when the new person didn't show up. We started at 7 a.m. and worked sometimes until after 9 p.m. to get everything done.

My girlfriend was a great help to me during this time. She helped me alleviate the stress. We just got away for a few hours. We talked or thought about something else during dinner or a movie.

We have 438 customers using our software to create, send, and track emails and newsletters to their subscribers. We are growing at about a 10 to 15 percent rate per month—not bad for a company that has been in business for a little over one year.

What I learned:

- When you are at the starting point, you know what your goal is but don't really have a path to getting there. You could wait until everything lines up perfectly (you have the financing in place, the product is perfect, and you have the team in place). Very rarely does everything come together before you start. Just start.
- We weren't really able to know everything we had to do in the beginning. We didn't really understand the market fully and didn't fully understand what people out there were looking for. We just had to take steps and then take a step back as we snowballed our way toward the learning curve.
- It is just persistence and getting a good team around you.

Applying the lessons learned to your business:

- Do your market research. If you are selling something that the market really isn't looking for or if you don't have a quality product, you can work your butt off for years and never really see a tangible result.
- Keep your ear to your customers and to the marketplace. The best way companies grow profitably is through referral and word of mouth sales. Follow up on all sales. Talk to your customers

at least once per quarter, more frequently if possible. This can be accomplished through personal contact, telephone calls, and surveys.

- Use educational newsletters to keep customers and potential customers up-to-date with new products and services. Always include material that will help them operate their business better. In addition, highlight current customers (with their permission) to show unique and different ways of using your current products and services. This helps your company "keep in touch" and increases sales.

#37

MY GUT TOLD ME SOMETHING WAS WRONG
Monica Y. Jackson

I was in the computer science industry for more than fifteen years and I worked for some large companies. I started getting very bored and decided to launch into computer consulting. I wanted to meet different organizations and companies, and work on different types of projects, as opposed to one specialized project.

I started writing columns and articles for many magazines and newspapers. A girlfriend said that she had a friend who was interested in starting a magazine. This man had established one in the past and I kept saying to myself, "I'm writing for all these magazines. Why don't I start my own?"

He and I met. He was very articulate, intelligent, and clean-cut. He appeared to be a very conservative man. I never bothered to check his background or anything else (like I normally do) because my friend, whom I had known for about eight years at the time, referred me to him. She had worked with him in the past.

I wanted to do something with a celebrity focus. The man she introduced to me brought a mock-up of a previous magazine that he had started. The mock-up of the magazine didn't fit his personality. It was cars and nearly nude women. He just didn't come across like that. That was red flag number one, but I missed it totally. I still felt that I was comfortable with him because I knew that this was something that I wanted to do and I knew that he had the knowledge to help me get where I wanted to go.

He made me an offer to be the freelance publisher and editor-in-chief of the magazine. I would provide all the content. Basically, it would be my magazine and he was just funding it. I accepted.

I actually wrote a contract for each individual story that I covered and he signed it. Each contract covered profiling the celebrity, fees for writing and editing, and traveling expenses.

I was about to go to Detroit, Michigan, to do an interview. He made all of the arrangements—air, hotel, and car. Upon getting ready to leave for the airport, I received a call informing me that the credit card had been declined. Immediately afterwards, I received a phone call that he would bring me the cash, because he didn't know what was going on with his credit card. I told him that I would cancel the interview if the arrangements were not taken care of. He drove to my house and gave me $1,200 in cash for the airfare and a portion of the car. Fortunately, the hotel was paid in full (on his sister's credit card, he

> *Follow your gut feeling even if someone seems intriguing and convincing.*

later told me). I got suspicious, but the feeling went away, since it was only about two hours before the plane's departure time.

The photo shoots and interviews for three celebrities went as planned. When I finish a job, I usually invoice immediately, but I was busy and didn't invoice him for about three weeks. I expected payment within thirty days, as per agreement. By this time, all the stories were complete.

Well, net thirty came and he hadn't paid. He said he had been really busy. By that time, I had to pay the editors, writers, photographers, and others who worked on the shoot with me. The invoice came to nearly $30,000.

In the meantime, I received a call that said, "Thank you for taking my job because I was offered the publisher and editor-in-chief positions first. I just want to let you know that this guy doesn't pay anybody."

I actually got on the phone and called the gentleman whom I was working with. I informed him that I received this phone call, and asked, "What is this about?" He said, "Oh that's just a disgruntled employee." So I said, "I haven't been paid so is there any truth in this?" My gut said there was.

I decided that I didn't want to deal with him and wrote him a letter dissolving our agreement. He kept calling and saying he didn't understand why I left the company this way. I told him I didn't really leave the company. I was a freelancer and I was not paid.

I decided to invest another $3,000 to print the magazine. I chose to spend more money on top of the $30,000 to produce my own magazine because I felt it was a credibility issue at that point. I didn't want to disappoint the celebrities, writers, or anyone else who worked on this project. To pay these people, I decided to sell my home as opposed to taking out a second mortgage on it.

What I learned:

- Pay attention to the yellow, orange, and red flags— they're always there in unscrupulous situations.
- Follow your gut feeling even if someone seems intriguing and convincing.
- I changed my invoicing policy. My policy now is 50 percent up front and 50 percent upon approval of the proof and before I print. My company now does

writing, editing, and graphics design. I am a stickler about how I invoice. I don't care if they are a large corporation or a repeat client because the fact of the matter is sometimes people forget or just become "slow pay" accounts and I don't want to deal with either.

- The magazine is now a showcase piece. I have definitely made back what I lost in more ways than one.

Applying the lessons learned to your business:

- Keep copies of all of the materials your company produces, including brochures, products, and services for clients, and media exposure. Many times, you can alter what was done for one client and use the concept or the model for another client. You never know when you will be able to use that material again.

- Keep track of your receivables. If your terms are net thirty, then if you haven't received a check by the 31st day, make a telephone call. Your client will know that you are serious about collecting your money. Your bookkeeper or other office person can do this. However, you must follow up to ensure that the telephone calls were made and learn the results of those telephone calls.

- In cases where you are invoicing a new customer for the first time, your accounts receivable person should call the accounts payable person for your customer, introduce herself, and find out what the format for getting invoices is. If you need specific signatures, copies of purchase orders, or other items, it is much better to know that before you bill than thirty days later when you make that telephone call. In addition, if there are collection issues later, it is much better to have an established working relationship with the customer prior to the problems arising.

#38

I DID IT ALL MYSELF
Pat Murphy

I grew up in the heating and air-conditioning business. My father started the business in 1952 and had my brother and me working in the business from the time we were five years old. I wanted to buy the business from my father. However, he insisted that I have my brother as a business partner. I refused since my brother was an alcoholic and was not productively working in the business. He was a detriment and I didn't need a boat anchor around my neck.

So, after many disagreements and ultimatums with my father, I started my own company on September 1, 1984. After all, I was thirty-four, young, and could do anything.

I had a degree in finance, knew how to price, and was educated technically. How hard could it be? I soon learned that it wasn't so easy.

On September 1, 1984, I was the sole employee. I had one customer: a Jersey City businessman who knew what I could do. So, I had work immediately, but unfortunately, with no money in the bank, I was extremely over-leveraged. That much I knew.

I kept asking myself, "Can you produce the work? Can you get the work done and get it done for the price that you prescribed?" If I was working a job by myself, I did fine. It was when I started to allocate work out that I encountered problems.

Naively I priced my jobs and service at the rate that it would have taken me to do the job. After all, I thought, everyone has the same work ethic that I have. I hired people assuming that they would work at the level they are supposed to (i.e., my speed and quality). That was a major mistake.

If you try to do everything yourself, you will end up in a dangerous sell-produce curve.

I spent a lot of time working at night. One job stands out in my mind. I went home, had dinner, and while watching my daughter's softball game, did all of the work necessary for a commercial building. The piping was totally laid out, the order was placed, and the materials were delivered. I gave it to one of my employees with the blueprint that I had laid out exactly the way I wanted the whole job done. Everything was there. I got to the job two days later and there were three times the amount of fittings there. He decided to change the way he was going to do it because he didn't bother following the paperwork. He decided he could do the job better his way and spent twice the amount of money.

So what did I do? I fired him. I said, "I don't need you changing what I've laid out and I can run this damn piping faster than you can." I proved to him, and maybe more to myself, that I could.

I was then in a no-win situation. I had to be on a job to get the work done, but I couldn't solicit more work because I had to be on a job. I was running in circles. I did the work well. However, I didn't have time to get more work to continue doing the work well. But if I delegated the work, it didn't get done well and the more work I got, the worse it was.

My wife did work in the office. Unfortunately, she struggled with the numbers and when the numbers didn't work, she wouldn't want to get me upset. So, she didn't show me the numbers. That turned into a snowball effect because I thought the numbers were fine and when I found the numbers weren't fine, I was in a huge hole.

I decided to shrink the company from ten to twelve employees down to two. This seemed to be the solution. However, it wasn't. I couldn't support myself with the debt load I had built as a ten- to twelve-person company.

We survived. But by the time I closed the business, we had at least a quarter million dollars in debt. I prayed a lot. I learned how hard it was to make the payroll, pay the taxes, interest payments, and everything else.

Every job that I took on was finished. Unfortunately, it did cost me the business.

The business lasted about ten years. I started phasing the business down about 1991 or 1992, full well knowing that I had been overly leveraged and was in debt up to my ears because of it. It just didn't make sense to continue. I had two children and I had to generate income. The business wasn't generating enough cash to eat and keep a roof over our heads. I started to teach and that led me down a very different path. In 2004, I paid the last of the debt off from the business.

What I learned:

- The most important asset of any company is its employees. At that time, twenty years ago, I was woefully inadequate at picking out my best assets. I did what everyone else did: I needed bodies, any bodies, whether they were good on the job or not. That is what creates most of the problems. The productivity just went down. You need the right employees in the right jobs.
- You need a support team.
- You have to have financial support.
- Would I start another business again? Yes, I would. But I would definitely do a lot more planning before I started it and I would not start one without the

proper financial support. And I would have a series of mentors that I could talk to.

Applying the lessons learned to your business:

- If you try to do everything yourself, you will end up in a dangerous sell-produce curve. You'll sell until you get a job, then produce the work. When it is done, there is nothing to do until you sell another job. When you are selling, you are not producing and when you are producing the work, you are not selling. This can burn you out and ultimately destroy your business.

- You need a continuous selling and marketing effort. This can be accomplished by an advertising and drip marketing program. Drip marketing is a regular, small, marketing activity that is sent to your customers every month. It could be an email, a postcard, a letter, or another form of advertising. The key is that it is continuous with a consistent message.

#39

I LOST 25 PERCENT OF MY BUSINESS IN ONE DAY
Karen Price
Safeguard Business Systems, Inc.

My mother was a Safeguard customer and her distributor was looking for part-time customer service help. So, I worked for him while I attended my first year of college. Then, I switched to working full time and took night classes in business, skipping all those seemingly silly basic courses.

As I watched the sales reps in the company earning significantly more than I was, I decided I wanted to sell. I did not finish a college degree and the only sales job I could find without the degree was life insurance sales. I was moderately successful at that for two years and got lots of sales training and experience. With both sets of grandparents owning businesses, I was always interested in having my own business.

When I decided to move to Atlanta, I was very interested in purchasing a Safeguard distributorship, but one was not available. So, I went to work for the corporate offices as a customer development manager. When the Atlanta territory became available, I purchased a portion of the existing accounts. Although there were people in upper management who did not think I could make it, I think they were glad to get me out of management as I don't play corporate politics well, and don't keep my mouth shut!

I finally had my own business. What propelled me in the beginning was the fact that some people didn't think I could do it. I began building the business to prove them wrong rather than for my own self-satisfaction.

One day I decided that it was stupid to build the business to prove that I could do it to the naysayers. I had to want to do it for me. I did. That's when I had my greatest challenge.

One of my customers represented $250,000 of my business. Their contract was up for renewal and Safeguard wanted to make changes that were unacceptable to the customer. Nothing I could do would make Safeguard keep the agreement as it was. So, in one day I lost $250,000 in business...more than 25 percent of my company's revenues.

I've made more on the bottom line with smaller customers.

I was absolutely furious. I was at the mercy of Safeguard and there was nothing I could do. I was a very small fish in a huge sea. I still wanted to eat and keep a roof over my head. And the business had to survive.

I had to scramble. I told the staff that it would be tight until I could replace that customer. Did they have any suggestions? It finally hit me that I had forgotten what had made me successful: hundreds of little customers rather than one big one. So, I contacted my current customers and prospected for others. I vowed never again would I let one customer control my business.

And, slowly, I rebuilt the customer base. In hindsight, I've made more on the bottom line with the smaller customers. And if one goes out of business, that doesn't affect me as much.

What I learned:

- Never let one customer represent more than 25 percent of your business.
- You've got to want a business for yourself; not to prove to others you can do it.
- After losing such a large customer and seeing the success in rebuilding the business with smaller customers, I decided that I would focus on smaller customers. We would deal with the repeat business that I could handle with my staff. I never want to be a million-dollar business again. We're profitable. I'm satisfied with my earnings and I want to stay small and in control.

Applying the lessons learned to your business:

- Winning your first large customer is exciting. Keeping that customer can be dangerous if that customer represents more than 20 percent of your revenues. The customer likes it because you'll pay a lot of attention to him. However, he can dictate terms and cause you to lose profitability.

- The danger with a customer representing more than 20 percent of your sales is that it usually takes time to replace a large customer. Sales cycles are long and finding a replacement could take months. Even if you have enough cash reserves, that reserve could be extinguished by the time you find another large customer.

- Once you get a large customer, find a second, a third, etc., so that any customer's business is less than 20 percent of your company's sales. Then, if any one customer leaves, your business is not in danger of failing.

#40

MY INDUSTRY WAS MALE DOMINATED
Billie Redmond
CEO, Coldwell Banker Commercial TradeMark Properties, Inc.

The real estate industry was once exclusively male dominated. When I first started, twenty years ago, there were no women in this business and for a long time it was all about men. Here's my story.

My father was a plumbing/general contractor and loved construction. So, I was used to the commercial side of business. I was working with a large mental health practitioner group as their business office manager, where several of the doctors were involved in real estate investments. I assisted them with their first office building development and realized how much I liked the process. I was hooked.

I met Don Watson and Alton Smith, two gentlemen who were both very established and well regarded in residential real estate. They wanted to start a commercial real estate firm and I agreed to join them in this venture. Together we began TradeMark Properties, now called Coldwell Banker Commercial TradeMark Properties, Inc.

Early on, I was forced to overcome the challenges of being a woman, and a petite woman at that. My size labeled me as easily intimidated and maneuvered. My competitors did not see me as someone to fear or someone to contend with, so they ignored me. That became an advantage.

Despite the competition ignoring me, I think my partners trusted me because they saw and believed in my strong work ethic. I deferred to them in making significant decisions and was good at communicating what was occurring. I knew when to go to them for their expertise and support and they knew that my motives were pure. They supported my decisions, even in the few cases where they thought I was wrong.

Payroll was always my greatest nightmare. In the beginning, I thought I was very close to closing the doors of my business. I was living "on the edge." Where was the cash going to come from? Fortunately, my partners kept reminding me that we were resilient and could make the tough decisions to get through the hard times.

In the early days, I rarely confided in my employees about the difficulties we were facing. However, I needed to let them know what was going on. This was the first conversation of many payroll nightmares that we had since we started the company.

I met with key employees and asked them for help. We discussed how we could stay away from that "edge" and what we could do together to ensure our survival. Without exception, they came through. They really are my family and there was just no way I was going to let them lose their jobs.

I brought in a management and business consultant that we had a strong relationship with. She sat down with me and reviewed the how and why of our situation. She helped me recognize the decisions that needed to be made. I knew what they were—I just didn't want to have to do what

You will make mistakes. Despite those mistakes, you can survive.

needed to be done. We developed a short-term business review process to help me see almost daily where we were. I'm happy to say we still use these processes today.

In many ways, I was a pioneer. It was hard to be taken seriously when everything you were born with—your gender, your physique—was working against you. You had to fight for your reputation as a professional and had to work twice as hard as someone with the luck of being male. Your work needed to be perfect because criticism was a constant factor.

I had perseverance on my side. I was fortunate enough to attract clients who were not gender biased. I worked with clients who wanted the best job done, regardless of sex. I had the perseverance to continue to demonstrate that we were the best in our industry and I worked hard to build our reputation and maintain it. I learned to deal with the payroll crises and as we grew, they became fewer and fewer.

With hard work and dedication to quality, we became successful and profitable. As a result, we had been approached to sell or merge the business with other firms. I didn't want to give up day-to-day control, so that always stopped us. The Coldwell Banker affiliation was perfect for us. We kept our own identity and have the ability to work within our market the way we know best. Yet, we have the national resources of one of the biggest and strongest commercial real estate brands behind us. It is a great partnership.

I am basically stubborn and that stubbornness translated into tenacity, persistence, and fear of failure. That fear of failure drove me to succeed in a market that was and still is dominated by men.

What I learned:

- You will make mistakes. Despite those mistakes, you can survive.

- Let people help you. There is a great deal of pride, loyalty, and commitment available when you accept help from others.

- My grandmother always told me that if you do the right thing, then right things would happen to you. If you are ever struggling to make a decision, flip a coin. Before it lands, you will be wishing for it to land one way or the other and you will know the answer. My grandmother was right. She was a brilliant woman.

Applying the lessons learned to your business:

- There are three types of businesspeople. The first type makes mistakes and doesn't learn from them. They are not very successful. The second type makes mistakes and learns from them. They represent the majority of businesspeople. The third type learns from the mistakes of others and never makes them. To be in this class, you must communicate with people in your business and learn from their wisdom. Read, take classes, join a group of noncompeting businesspeople. You'll still make mistakes. However, they won't be the mistakes others have made. And when you make them, you'll have people around you to help correct the errors.

- Don't be afraid to be the first in your area to do something. If you are unique, then you have a great public relations angle and are likely to be featured in the press. However, make sure that it is the media outlets that your customers watch, listen to, and read.

#41

THE BOTTOM DROPPED OUT OF THE MARKET
Anonymous

My husband and I purchased a manufacturing business. As an engineer, he was responsible for making sure that the manufacturing processes worked and I handled the sales, marketing, and financial aspects of the company.

We grew the business into a multimillion-dollar business by producing high-end specialty products for the medical device and biotech markets. Known as the experts in this field, we have attracted *Fortune* 500 companies who became clients.

One of our *Fortune* 500 customers awarded us several million dollars of work. We invested about $1.5 million in new equipment and raw materials for the molds. We hired and ramped up to serve their needs. Then, unexpectedly, the bottom dropped out of their market and the *Fortune* 500 company didn't order any parts.

We sat with equipment, raw materials, employees, and payments to make on the equipment. The customer couldn't order from anyone else because we had their custom molds. No one was ordering from any manufacturer in that market. The chip business had dried up. We suffered for fourteen months.

Through that process, we made a conscious decision to keep all of our permanent staff. We let temporary labor go. This sent a message to our employees that they were more valuable than the temporary labor. We felt that if we lost that collective expertise, it would be tough to rebuild it.

To be able to do this, we cut out all shift differential payments to second and graveyard shifts. We reduced everyone's salary 20 percent for three months and my husband and I took no salary for over a year.

We kept all permanent employees for two main reasons. First, they had been part of our success for fifteen years, almost seeming like family. They are a big part of our future. Second, they embody so much knowledge that if they weren't here when we did ramp up, it would be very difficult starting again.

With every paycheck I sent out a memo so employees knew what was going on in the company, what business we won, what challenges we were facing, and what action we were taking. I continue to do that every two weeks even now that the crisis is over because I think it eliminates what I call "water cooler talk." The rumor mill doesn't fly so rapidly. If I don't state what's actually going on, then they are just going to make it up.

We continued to not take a paycheck for more than fourteen months so that the company could post a year-end profit. We could have posted a loss last year and everyone would have understood. However, I have such a close relationship with our bank that I wasn't willing to do that. It jeopardizes our future requests with them for new equipment requests or an increased line of credit. The bank knew what actions we were taking to do that because I make sure I keep them included.

My husband and I worked out and walked every night. This helped because we were in it together and could support each other. In addition, I pulled weeds and tended the flowers. A minimum of a handful a day of weeds gets rid of the stress.

We made sure we surrounded ourselves with friends. Some were in similar situations and some were not. They could hold us to a higher standard and help us remember in the dark days that the good days are around the corner because this is a cyclical business.

It was scary because this was the first time we took no salary for over a year. We prayed a lot and we kept closely coupled to our customers so that we made sure no customers jumped ship.

Communicate with your employees when the bad times come.

No one thought it would last a year. We continued to make loan payments. We were sitting on very expensive inventory that couldn't be used for our other projects. It was frustrating because we knew it was a matter of time before they started ordering.

My fellow manufacturers suffered for three years, so I told our employees that as much as it was painful for us, we at least had jobs. We had other customers that were ordering and we all knew we would have a future. This business would come back—the question was how long would it take? So we just had to keep reminding people, our staff, why we were here, what we were doing, and that it would turn around. When the good times happened, then we would start seeing some better results.

The good times did come back. During the very difficult eighteen months, we made all of our loan payments, kept our employees, and still had our banking relationships. We never hiccuped with the landlord, our vendors got paid, and our toolmakers got paid. We just made sure everyone else was taken care of, but we made other people aware that it was tough on us. Many of our friends didn't have the will to survive and went out of business.

What I learned:

- Communicate with your employees when the bad times come. Even more so then. Everyone took a salary hit and we led by example.
- A supportive husband and friends are important. They helped us with perspective when the bad times hit.
- You have to have the will to survive. Exercise and pulling weeds help get rid of the stress.
- Keep your sense of humor.

Applying the lessons learned to your business:

- Everyone should share in the good times and the bad times. Never ask your employees to do something that you aren't doing. This means that when salary cuts are necessary, you should take the largest salary cut. If you are taking no salary, employees will wonder how you are paying your personal bills. Explain in overall terms that you are living from your savings.

- In good times, share the profits with your employees. Everyone participated and worked toward earning those profits. Establish a profit-sharing plan. Everyone should understand how the profits are generated and how they are distributed. You don't have to teach the employees the details of reading financial statements. However, they should have a basic understanding of how their jobs affect revenues and expenses. Many times they will have suggestions on ways to increase revenues and decrease expenses once they understand the relationship between their jobs, overhead, and revenue.

#42

I WANTED TO BE THE HERO
Anonymous

I had been working for a large corporation for seventeen years and even though I was successful, I finally realized that I wasn't going to get what I wanted by working for somebody else. I decided to look for a business to buy. I talked to brokers and looked at several opportunities. Nothing felt right.

Then one day I saw an ad in the Sunday paper about a tremendous hot tub business that needed somebody really capable to help it get out of bankruptcy. The ad got my attention. I could help. The owner had moved the operations from California to Washington.

I was naive enough to think that having been successful working for a corporation meant a lot when it came to understanding what it takes running a small business… especially one that has problems enough to get it into bankruptcy. I was just full of excitement. I thought I could be the hero.

As a result, I overlooked all the obvious things. The worst was the fact that the guy who was looking for a business partner was the one who drove the company into bankruptcy in the first place. I ignored every signal that there possibly could have been. I ignored my friends' and wife's comments about what they saw. I just wanted to do this.

My wife definitely told me not to do it and my friends were openly skeptical. But to me, they didn't see it the right way. I had money in retirement assets and savings. I also borrowed some money from my family and got the company going. I was going to rescue the business!

We had a handshake deal. I was president of the company. The stock was split 50/50. I didn't seek anyone's advice. I didn't bother with an accounting system. We had no books or financial statements. I just wanted to jump in and get us on the right track.

We started by making a hot tub and selling at retail. We took the cash from that sale and made another one. We sold it and used the cash to make two. We sold those and made four.

I started getting suspicious three or four months into the game. My father, who is an accountant, was asking me questions about his personal investment. I didn't have good answers, but still I totally ignored everything... including the advice of my father. I couldn't believe that anything would spoil my dream.

My wife was correctly cautious and angry with me continually dipping into assets. When things would get tight, I would put more money in. My partner played me perfectly. He would say, "We are going to be out of business on Friday unless we put an ad in the paper and get some leads."

Since my father didn't like my answers, he decided to see what was going on for himself. He traveled across the country to visit our operation and he was shocked that there were no books. He started putting the books together.

He showed me the discrepancies. I still didn't do anything. Then, wisely, my father asked for his money back. I gave it to him. Even *that* didn't shake my misguided faith.

As sales quickly increased and the business grew, I could no longer do the little bit of watching that I was doing. I was paying all the bills and trying to learn the production side of the business. I was worrying about leads, people management, and growth.

The death knell was when I gave my business partner the ability to sign checks. Our growth exploded...as did our liabilities...*my* liabilities.

In one year, the company sold almost $1 million worth of hot tubs. After I gave him the ability to sign checks, we never paid taxes. We didn't pay our advertising bills. Some people never got their hot tubs. At one point there were forty people working for us. It was a nightmare.

Your business will suffer or fail whenever your ego gets in the way.

My business partner disappeared. It turned out I never knew his true name. I didn't even have his right social security number.

I tried to sell the company after my "business partner" disappeared. I got close, but couldn't put it together. I put the company in bankruptcy and dissolved the corporation. It took me with it.

During this whole process, I kept dipping into savings and cashing in assets. I ended up with a lot of personal guarantees when the business was all done. I was sued by more creditors than I knew I had, and it forced me into a personal Chapter 13. That whole journey took about two years. I paid off what I negotiated in the Chapter 13 in about a year and a half.

What I learned:

- Don't become emotionally involved. I had a dream and it was completely naive. I've always had a hero-type personality. This is my ideal personal image. As a kid, I watched all the cowboy movies and I always figured I was the guy coming in on the white horse, rescuing the pretty girl, and killing the bad guys. I'd find the gold and everyone would live happily ever after. This was perfection for me, and my former partner knew it. I didn't allow myself to see obvious things because I didn't want the vision to be destroyed.
- I continuously made bad decisions and I am totally accountable for everything that I did. I made those decisions because I didn't want it to fail. I always felt it would work out somehow. A business needs plans. It needs checks and balances. It needs financial controls.
- Don't give a partner the ability to sign checks to spend your money. Never.

Applying the lessons learned to your business:

- Your business will suffer or fail whenever your ego gets in the way. Ego has no place in business decisions.
- You must have accurate monthly financial statements. This is the way you keep score. This is the way that you spot minor issues before they become major crises. This is the way you track increasing or decreasing profitability.
- Small changes in margins are warning signs of impending losses or bad jobs. Usually these small changes are not detected unless you receive financial statements each month. Take steps to eliminate the problems.
- Many times the reason for not having financial statements is that an owner does not want to know how bad things are. However, for the company to survive, you need to know where it stands financially. Once you get an accurate baseline, no matter how bad it is, you can plan and implement changes that will move the company towards profitability.

#43

TOO MUCH OF A GOOD THING
Loretta Elbel

In the early 1990s, we had a contract to supply the government with computer software. As a small, women-owned business, we were one of the few with this type of contract. Microsoft came to us asking us to offer a special on Microsoft Office to the Department of Defense agencies since, at that time, WordPerfect was the word processor of choice in government offices. It would be a white package bought directly from Microsoft and not through our usual sources. Since it was late in the fiscal year, we quickly sent out mailers and Microsoft alerted their government representatives. We expected $100,000 to $200,000 in orders. I came to the office one Saturday soon after the special was offered and found over $1 million in orders.

This was a major problem. Why? I had over $2 million in orders in addition to the other end of year orders for software and hardware. Microsoft's credit limit on new accounts was $50,000, no matter who you were, who your customers were, or what your credit was like. Our line of credit was tapped out. The government paid in sixty to ninety days and Microsoft wanted their money in thirty days or less. Even worse, once you reached your credit limit with Microsoft, there were no more shipments until you were under the credit limit. Period.

This put enormous stress on me. We prided ourselves on great customer service and quick deliveries. We needed to keep the government contract. Where was I going to get the money to fill the orders? I went out to my car, opened the sunroof, and drove away, screaming at the top of my lungs.

Once that was out of me, my brain started to function again. First, prioritize the orders. Who was most important? It was all the government. I made a list of who got their software first, second, third, etc.

Second, where could I find some short-term cash? Our line of credit was tapped out and the likelihood of increasing it was slim to none. Next thought? Family. I borrowed money from my sister...not enough, but it helped.

Third, I wrote letters to the lowest government customers on my priority list: Due to unforeseen order volume, expect ship- ment of your product in thirty to sixty days. This was much longer than our normal one- to two-week turnaround. We had a few people complain, but not many. Most accepted the letter and appreciated that we sent it to let them know when to expect the software.

Screaming at the top of your lungs is a short-term solution.

Fourth, we got on the telephone and collected receivables as fast as we could. It was useless to call the government receivables. At that time, they paid in sixty to ninety days no matter what. The quick payment legislation had not been enacted yet. However, all of our other customers who were approaching thirty days or past thirty days were called and politely asked when we could expect payment. By making those telephone calls, we got some cash in faster than it would have come in. That cash immediately went to Microsoft to order more products to be shipped to government customers.

This whole process took about four months. It got to the point where I didn't want to open the mail and see more orders. The stress of being too successful, the huge orders without the ability to have the cash to fulfill the orders, was immense.

I spent a lot more time in my car with the roof open, screaming. It helped. Being honest with our customers, being on top of receivables, and prioritizing orders helped more.

What I learned:

- A "special" that is too successful can be bad.
- If you think that you have enough of a credit line and enough cash, you probably don't.
- Screaming at the top of your lungs is a short-term solution. You have to have a plan to get through the cash crunch.

Applying the lessons learned to your business:

- Always test your advertising activities on a small sample. If you find that the ad is not successful, you won't waste a lot of money on media that doesn't work. If you find the ad is very successful, you can plan the roll out of the ad so that you have enough product to cover the orders. The roll out may take longer than you had initially planned. However, you won't disappoint customers and you won't have a cash shortfall.
- Apply for the largest line of credit that you can get. In most cases, you won't be charged for the line until you use it. Then, when a large order or other cash crunch comes, you have access to cash.

#44

MY DISTRIBUTOR WENT BANKRUPT
Adria Manary
CEO, *Magic of Life Enterprises*

Independent Publishers Magazine calls me the Energizer Bunny because no matter what happens, I keep coming back.

I'm passionate about what I do. However, the same passion that has kept me going, has sometimes gotten me in trouble. I grew up in Washington, D.C., and followed political families. I was prepared when I was offered the opportunity to write a book about America's royal family: *Kennedys: The Next Generation*. I was so excited to be working with a large publisher and having a book to my credit that I didn't negotiate a decent contract. Long story short, the publisher went bankrupt, and I didn't receive money owed on my contract or the rights to my materials.

When I realized there was nothing I could do about the situation, I decided to write about something I loved. The second book was a poetry book, *Touched by a Rainbow*. I quickly learned that although my friends and family loved it, there was no market for this book.

I was a journalism major in college and had been writing since I was a child. It was time to get serious. I did research on how to market books. I was married with three children and found out that writing about what you love has great value. My son named my third book *Mommy Magic*. This time, thinking I had learned my lesson, I self-published the book and found a distributor.

I did my research on the distributor I was interested in. A friend had sold 100,000 books through them and was always paid. However, they too filed bankruptcy and I couldn't retrieve my books. I cried until there were no more tears left.

I went into hibernation for two years. I wanted out of writing. I wanted to do something different. My dad had owned a retail store for forty-two years. Was retailing for me? I bought a children's boutique in Carlsbad. I rationalized. Since I loved children, what could be better? I didn't do my due diligence. I just wanted out of what I had been through. Besides, I had done my homework before and lost in the end.

I saw what I wanted to see and didn't dig. I thought I was going into a profitable business. It wasn't. To make matters worse, the owner stole from the business. I resorted to calling the police to get my merchandise back. The business lasted about a year. I knew that retailing wasn't for me. What was?

At this point, I thought I was a magnet for bad luck. Could anything go right? One night someone called me and she was starting a company called Books and Beyond. It was a catalog company that sold books much like

Stick with your passion; if you try something else, you won't succeed.

the one I wrote. She was planning to host home parties. She ordered and paid for several thousand books. Believe it or not, they also went bankrupt. However, at least I got paid for these. Perhaps my luck was changing.

What kept me going through all of this? I realized that my passion is writing. Retailing isn't for me. I've written since I was a child. My whole purpose is to spread love. That's what I do best and enjoy most. I am tenacious and didn't want to give up. Looking back, the reality was that I could have made the retail shop work if I had wanted to. I didn't. I just wanted to write.

I know what I want and what I need. Will I find another outlet for the book? I don't know. What I do know is that I'll never stop trying!

What I learned:

- The people that win are the people who get through the tough times, put it behind them, and still go on.
- Stick with your passion; if you try something else, your heart won't be in it and it won't succeed.

Applying the lessons learned to your business:

- Sometimes it takes years of struggle before your company is successful. If you believe in what you are doing and are serving a growing number of customers, you are building your business. Small steps toward profitability will eventually get you there.

#45

STRESS FROM AN UNEXPECTED PLACE
Rochele Hirsch
CEO, *CommExpress*

Leaving my successful fifteen-year corporate career with a major telecommunications company surprised many people. Along with the President's Club Award, I was interviewed for the next issue of the company magazine as one of the top seven women movers-and-shakers. However, the idea of continuing to put my energy into a company that, in my mind, seemed to have little concern about effective operations didn't fit my sense of success. I needed to find out what I really wanted to do with my life.

The first major step I took after leaving the company was to attend a program called STAR. Founded by Barbara Findeisen, this powerful three-week intensive program connected the "rational" understanding of my life's history with the emotions that had never been expressed. I learned how to unravel and defuse the stress-drivers in my life. I regained my passion and sense of joy. I was ready to start working again.

After five months of vacation, I began my independent consulting practice, working with corporate, government, and education leaders on issues of organization effectiveness and business development. Over the years, income from my consulting projects also helped support several entrepreneurial business ventures, from real estate renovation to software development. In 1994, my consulting work took me to a project in Singapore. One project turned into two, and then to three. I had decided to stay on for another year, just as the third project was cancelled.

Rather than giving up and going home, I turned my attention to another venture, different from the organization consulting. New friends in Singapore had encouraged me to turn my hobby, personal color analysis, into a business there. So, I developed the business plan and launched the venture. Despite excellent press, some good clients, and exciting seminars, the revenue was not enough to live in this expensive city. Before leaving for a visit to Atlanta, I moved out of the house I could no longer afford, and stored my things with friends.

The next five weeks in Atlanta added to my distress. I came back to Singapore with my right hand in a cast, dealing with the break-down of a relationship, real estate business problems at home, and not knowing where my *Many times business owners cause their own problems.* next dime was coming from. Fortunately, I was able to house-sit for some friends. But I was beside myself. I had no income, no projects, and no prospects for enough money to stay.

My anxiety was getting the best of me. My "rational" efforts were going nowhere, I wasn't sleeping, and I didn't know what to do better. From my experience in emotional healing work, I knew that anxiety is something you cannot deal with directly. It is a tangle of emotions that causes you to feel impending doom—and it blocks the flow of life. To defuse the anxiety, the component emotions, such as fear and hurt, must be untangled and worked with separately.

So one night around midnight, I decided I had had enough. I was ready to untangle the mess. To do this, I had to dive into the emotions. So, I started crying and beating pillows—really heating up the "sludge"—to discover what needed healing. Anger, fear, hurt, shame, self-blame, fury, what's wrong with me...the words came tumbling out. I continued to keep the bonfire of emotions going. And then these words came through loud and clear: "I am afraid of disappointing my mother and my brother." Okay, so what? Tell me more. "Then they won't love me...and if they don't love me...I'll die!" There, I had it. My fear, the root of my anxiety, was not about having no money, a potential bankruptcy, or failing in my business. It was about disappointing my mother and brother, my subconscious source of love, what I needed to survive.

I knew that such a survival belief was not logical, but it was real, and it was a driver in my life. While it was hidden from my awareness, I couldn't do anything about it. I just felt completely stressed. But now that I saw it, I could change. My "adult" knows that my true source of love—of energy—is not from my mother and brother... it is from the Eternal. So I shifted. I transformed my two-year-old's survival fear of losing their love into a celebration of feeling the love that is always there.

Next, I pulled out a book of Zen sayings and opened to: "There are no guarantees in life...except that it is an adventure."

I asked myself, "What is my worst case scenario? Bankruptcy? Well then, it is just another part of the adventure. Like having high tides and low tides. I'm okay in any tide...it is just a different experience."

With that thought in mind—and in body—I felt safe to ride through this adventure and watch how it turned out. My stress dropped and I could feel the flow of life.

Within three days, I had a new project. It was as if a gate had opened and money started coming in. I was doing work that I loved, and I could continue as an entrepreneur. It proved, once again, that my true safety begins within myself—not from what I do.

What I learned:

- While it is easy to blame stress and anxiety on current circumstances, I find that the true stress points run much deeper and are not so logical. Along with my consulting work and my business ventures, much of my attention during the last fifteen years has been on transformational healing. The catalyst for some of my greatest breakthroughs has come from being financially "close to the edge."

- One focus of my journey has been about pushing the career envelope. Rather than taking a safe "success route" for me (i.e., going for a thirty-year corporate career), I've used my "high-tide, low-tide" adventures as an entrepreneur to give me both the opportunity to design and develop my ideas, and to use the stressful times for healing and transforming. I continue to gain more freedom, more choice, more passion, *and* more success. It's a great life!

Applying the lessons learned to your business:

- Many times business owners cause their own problems. I've worked with companies and helped them out of crises. I left them in good shape. A year later, they were back in the same poor condition and many times in worse shape. What I found was that the owners sabotaged their success. They got bored or tried to change things that were working properly.
- When you become successful, don't try to change things that are working unless a competitor, the market, or the economy forces you to change. If you don't have as much to do, find a charitable cause that you can support and work with that organization. Give back to the community and enjoy the fruits of your success!

#46

I DIDN'T WATCH THE BOOKS
Maureen Mitchell
CEO, Advanced Technology Services/Optidoc

We walked out of the attorney's office stunned. Neither my partner, who had invested money in the business, nor I could say a word on the drive back to the office. The - bankruptcy attorney had described, in vivid detail, what it was like to go through bankruptcy. I was speechless. At that moment, I knew I had to do something else. Bankruptcy was not an option. I couldn't go through it. There had to be another way to climb out of this $700,000 hole I had dug us into, since failure was not an option either.

How did we get into this mess? We wanted to grow the business. I wanted to concentrate on my strength, selling. I searched for and hired a person who supposedly had the ability to grow the company. Great references.

When it's your business, you can't abdicate overall responsibility.

Bad manager. I kept my titles of chairman of the board and president. I gave him the title of CEO and free rein to operate the business.

That was a mistake. He spent money on everything. Why not? It wasn't his money. Everyone got new equipment. He hired a recruiting firm to find people and paid high fees that we couldn't afford. He hired "yes people." He didn't pay payroll taxes. He got us into debt that we couldn't handle.

To make matters worse, he cooked the books. Part of his compensation was a bonus based on results and he made sure he got a bonus.

Where was I while all of this was happening? I was happily doing what I loved. I was selling and bringing work in the door. However, I wasn't bringing enough business fast enough to cover the money that we were spending. I didn't have a clue what was really going on.

I realized that we were in a lot of trouble when the CEO tried to sell a piece of the company to a third party, and was going to sell me, too. He started talking about employment contracts and included an employment contract for me. There was no way that I was going to sell out. Until he made that mistake, I had no idea how bad we were. I started digging.

When he tried to sell me with the company, I immediately fired him and started running the business again. I had the books audited. Imagine my surprise when we were hundreds of thousands of dollars in debt and owed the Internal Revenue Service for payroll taxes.

We laid off personnel. I personally called all of the creditors. I got my butt in gear and really started selling hard. That's what I always wanted to do anyway. Now I had a critical reason to do it.

As an entrepreneur, I knew that I couldn't fail. I had to do what it takes to get through this mess. I knew that we have a niche in the software market and blue chip clients. Unfortunately, the sales cycle is long. However, when clients use our programs and become more efficient, they return over and over again. I started going back to existing customers for more work and asking for referrals. It worked.

We are still digging out of the hole four years later. I'm still selling. However, I am watching the financial statements. The business is stable and profits are increasing.

What I learned:

- When it's your business, you can't abdicate overall responsibility. You can't abdicate the checkbook.
- You can get through the tough times with a great product and sales ability. You have to sell a problem solution. You have to show your customers that you can show them how to save time and money.
- React quickly, even if it is difficult.

Applying the lessons learned to your business:

- Profitable sales are one of the best ways to solve your cash needs when you are in a cash crunch. Go to your existing customers and offer them additional products and services. If your normal payment terms are net thirty, offer a discount for payment up front. Just make sure that the discount isn't so steep that it causes the sale of those products to be unprofitable.
- Once the initial cash crisis is over, grow your cash reserves to at least six weeks of payroll. This should give your company enough cushion to handle late receivables.
- Another way to lessen a cash crunch is to consider changing your payment policies. Consider requiring a down payment, cash prior to shipping, or progress payments.

#47

MY CUSTOMER SAID HE WOULDN'T PAY US

Steve Saunders
CEO, *Tempo Mechanical, Inc.*

I never thought that I would be an entrepreneur. I was content. I was enjoying running a division for TD Industries, a construction company that consistently makes it to the top ten *Fortune Magazine* best companies to work for list. It is a great company to work for and I had worked my way up over the past twelve years. One day in 1998, I was given a choice: either spin off the division into its own separate company or TD Industries would shut it down. Personally, I knew that I would be okay either way. But I felt an obligation to the people who were working with me. I knew that some of them wouldn't be okay without a job. So, I made the choice to become an entrepreneur...a choice that I never dreamed that I would have to make.

I got a crash course in entrepreneurship even before I was the official president. I was the only person required to give a personal guarantee. Since I was a "happy-go-lucky" kind of guy, I thought, "no big deal." After I made the decision, there was a two-month period before the paperwork was signed.

I discovered that our division, soon to be a new company, was in chaos and I was going to be responsible.

The financials showed for this two-month period that the business was unsustainable. And I was signing a personal guarantee for a potentially bankrupt business. I had visions of losing everything I owned.

This two-month period was right in the middle of a computer software change so I didn't know whether it was software glitches or that the huge losses were real. On top of the financials, the departments were out of control. There was two to three times more business than the people could handle and the company was giving work back to the customers saying they couldn't handle it.

In the back of my mind, I knew there was still time to get out of the deal since the final paperwork hadn't been signed. Stress? I took my blood pressure every night for two months during the transition and it was incredibly high. I didn't show the stress on the outside, but I was definitely experiencing it on the inside. The "happy-go-lucky guy" wasn't so happy-go-lucky. I knew it, but my team didn't see it.

Curiously, the day I signed the papers (including the personal guarantee) and became president of Tempo Mechanical (our new company name), my blood pressure went back to normal and stayed there. I didn't know why. Finally, I realized that at long last I had the power to control my own destiny. I would be sinking or swimming on my own merit. I had a sense of calm and began to manage the new business. Things got better, in fact, much better.

I didn't know how close I would come to sinking. It looked like 2001 would be a good year for Tempo Mechanical. We had outgrown our space in the past three years and were searching for a building to purchase. The company purchased it on July 15, 2001. Business was good and we decided to completely renovate it using our line of credit. After all, we were profitable, we had cash, and we had never needed the line of credit. To top it off, our forecasts showed that we wouldn't. The business was running profitably.

September 11, 2001, hit and business stopped. It was too late to cut back on expenses since the move was scheduled for September 15, 2001. We moved in on October 15, 2001, and despite extreme coordination and planning, we had four days without telephones. The week after we moved in, I got a letter from a builder customer that stated, "We can't pay the $750,000 we owe you. We won't ever be able to pay you and hope that this doesn't hurt you." Were they kidding?

Sometimes you have to take educated risks.

I considered my options. I told the partners (Tempo Mechanical is an ESOP, which means that employees own a piece of the business and are called partners) and asked for suggestions.

The company had used up its line of credit renovating the building. I went to the bank and asked for an increase in our line of credit...after all, the bank had offered to do it once before. The bank's answer: we'll give you one dollar in credit for every two dollars you give us in assets. It surprised, no shocked, me. Okay, I thought, what's next? Tempo had to have cash for payroll and to purchase materials for our jobs.

We renegotiated with suppliers for longer terms. Now most of our suppliers were paid in sixty days rather than thirty days.

We were creative in other ways as well. We refinanced everything we could, including the new sprinkler system and our existing fleet of trucks. I had to raise cash. The interest rate didn't matter. I just needed the cash. The focus was on survival. With cash and no profits, you have a business. With profits and no cash, you are out of business.

I could have, and perhaps should have, laid off a third of the company that December. However, they were and are good, loyal people and partners in the company. I realized that the company can suffer financial reverses and I wouldn't get the people back after they left. So, everyone stayed.

It was time to pressure the builder. As the houses came close to the lien dates, we would make a call. We need "$X" by Friday or we will file a lien. In the beginning, we got little pieces of what was owed.

One Friday, the builder told me that they would have to file bankruptcy if they paid us. So, therefore, they simply would not pay any more money. My retort: "If you don't pay, then we are going down. So, we are filing the liens immediately and you can go into bankruptcy with us." At that moment, when the words came out of my mouth, I realized how much of an entrepreneur I had become. I was a risk taker.

We got paid the entire $750,000 over a period of ten months. We made payroll every week, sometimes by the skin of our teeth. We paid all of our suppliers within the renegotiated terms, all of the back bonuses, and other liabilities as business picked up.

What I learned:

- Through strength of will, you can survive.
- Good news isn't usually as good as it sounds and bad news isn't usually as bad as it sounds.
- Creativity and communications are critical. Seek help early. Everyone in the company and our banker knew most everything. They all came up with some great ideas on how to raise cash.
- I used to be a jovial, happy guy. I'm still like that on the outside, but I have a much harder shell on the inside. I am an entrepreneur.

Applying the lessons learned to your business:

- Sometimes you have to take educated risks. Do your homework. Try to determine all of the unintended consequences of your actions. Once you have planned what needs to be done, then execute that plan.

- Cash flow is critical for survival. At the end of every week, you need to know the beginning cash on hand, what came into the company through collection on sales and other sources, and what checks you wrote to determine the ending balance for the week. Then you need to estimate the cash needs and influx for the following week to ensure that you have enough to cover payroll and your other expenses. If you don't have enough to cover payroll, it is better to know it a week ahead to put efforts into collecting money so that there will be enough cash to cover your operating needs for that week.

#48

OUR CAUSE CAN'T BE CHEAP
Thomas Kemper
CEO, Dolphin Blue, Inc. — Dallas, Texas

I grew up near Times Beach, Missouri. The diseases and the environmental devastation that occurred in both Times Beach and Fenton, my hometown, affected me profoundly. I decided that I had to make a difference in the world and do whatever I could to preserve the natural resources of this planet for future generations.

At the Dallas Shakespeare Festival, I noticed that there were a lot of recyclable commodities, or resources, being dumped in the trash after each evening's performance. I approached the organizers of the event and asked to start a recycling program. They agreed. I very quickly found that recycling doesn't work very well. I was shocked to learn that most of the time the supposed recyclable materials still end up in landfills or waste-to-energy incinerators. It costs a lot to transport recyclable goods. Because of the subsidizing of virgin-material goods, there really isn't much of an incentive to create markets for recycled products.

It hit me that the only way recycling is going to work is when we buy products made from materials we attempt to recycle. I started Dolphin Blue, Inc., to sell products made from, or partially made from, recycled materials. As much as I delight in what I am doing, it's been scary since the beginning.

We compete against office giants like Staples and Office Depot and we get compared in every arena and always on price. It is frustrating because as a small business, we don't have the purchasing power. We're competing by sending our message in a way that people will say "I'm paying for those cheap products anyway (in the form of tax-supported cleanup of water, air, and loss of resources), so I ought to be buying products that are less polluting and create a sustainable planet." It's a tough message to get across.

Many times you have to start small, even if you have big goals.

It's funny. People will save for college for their kids with the intent that it is going to create a better life for that kid and their children. But what about the air they breathe, the water they drink, the quality of their food, and just the quality of the planet? Why aren't we investing in that?

We are changing people's focus. It is exceedingly difficult. The change is almost imperceptible at times. The rewards are few and I get frustrated at the pace of change. However, I rarely show the frustration because I enjoy leading a very dedicated group of employees who believe in what I am committed to doing. If I'm frustrated, they will become frustrated.

We are trying to become profitable and we're struggling in doing so. There are days that I feel as if I don't know how much longer I can do it. We compete in a marketplace where there is so much emphasis on price, on invoice value as opposed to sustainability and environmental or social value.

My wife left me. I came home July 19, 2002, and the house was empty and she was gone. She had been part of the business. Her comment: "You are married to this business and you won't see anything but making this business succeed."

I was in shock. She said she was just so scared because we were always on the brink and she didn't want to be part of the crash. Her way of dealing with it was to just exit. It threw me into a tailspin for about six months.

Yet I persisted. I believed in what I was doing and I had to keep going. I had trusted her to do the books and had to find someone to replace her. I hired someone who had been working in a *Fortune* 500 company and was highly compensated. She was very highly qualified. I saw her skills, the acumen she brought to the table, and I knew this was someone I needed to help me grow my business. I paid her almost as much as I paid myself. It was significantly less than she was making at the *Fortune* 500 company. She had lost her position there because the CEO had run the business into bankruptcy. She was part of a 900-employee layoff. Her employment with us lasted barely eighteen months. She couldn't handle a small business environment where we were continually struggling to make ends meet and she perceived she had no room to grow.

Others look at why have I hung in there and say, "Why are you doing it?" In this vein, I recall a conversation with my banker one day when he said to me, "Your prices are higher than Staples and Office Depot, so why are you doing this?" I said, "We have kids that you and I may never know—a couple of generations down the pipe—and what kind of world are we going to leave them if someone doesn't take a stand and do the kind of things I'm doing? It doesn't matter if it's a guy selling recycled office supplies or some guy in the electric motor business selling highly efficient electric motors or the guy selling hybrid cars, we are doing it because we believe in something. We're standing against the drift, swimming 'upstream' against the current. I look at the fact that there are 600,000 school-age children in this country that are using inhalers and that's not right."

The banker sat in silence. He looked at me and said, "I never thought about that. I coach ten-year-old boys in soccer games and suddenly they are gasping for air. Ten out of twelve have inhalers." After a moment he then said, "I think I now understand why you do this."

Despite the financial fear, my wife leaving me, and all of the other trials and tribulations I have been through, I know that my business will succeed. It was a choice I made and I will see it happen.

What I learned:

- Belief in myself, why I am doing what I am doing, will get me through to achieve my life's goals.
- We all need someone we can lean on in the tough times.
- I need to continue setting and achieving goals. The future? Build a small recycled paper mill in Dallas, Texas, as a model that can be duplicated nationwide and globally.

Applying the lessons learned to your business:

- As I've written in previous stories, business planning and executing that plan are critical to your success.

Find outsiders who have your business interest at heart and help keep you on track. Business owners have very few people to answer to. If you take your outsiders' interest seriously, then you have someone to answer to who will keep you on track.

- Many times you have to start small, even if you have big goals. Create a model that works in an area and replicate that model in other areas. Make sure that you have enough cash to replicate the models before you begin. You can grow your company out of business by not having enough cash to sustain the growth.

#49

I COULDN'T BUILD A COMPANY FOR MY IDEA

David Moskowitz, MD, FACP

Chairman, CEO and Chief Medical Officer, GenoMed, Inc.

It really began a dark and stormy night about eleven years ago, around Halloween, 1993. I just assumed I would spend my entire life in academics. I was training then as a kidney doctor. My project from about 1984 was to find the trigger that makes people's kidneys grow. When you take out one kidney, the other kidney always grows. No matter what animal species you belong to, it always happens.

I was obsessed with finding the trigger so that the people who were headed toward dialysis could grow bigger kidneys and stay off dialysis for a little while longer. I started working on the project in 1984. About nine years later, in 1993, as I was writing yet another grant, I suddenly realized what the trigger was: angiotensin II.

I realized something more at that moment. This signal for growth, angiotensin II, was making the kidneys fail. It took a few more years to understand that a growth factor that keeps driving cells to form more cells ultimately drives those cells to commit suicide. That is, if they're polite and do the right thing. In fact, it is the impolite cells that escape from growth control and form cancers. Cells have only two choices when constantly pressured by a growth factor like angiotensin II. The kidneys were failing because their cells were all polite and just committing suicide in the face of continued pressure from angiotensin II to keep growing.

So, in 1993, I already had a cure for kidney failure. The startling fact was that the perfect drugs for blocking angiotensin II, called ACE inhibitors, had already been around for twenty-five years. They are safe and very well known drugs.

I tried getting funding from everywhere I could, including the drug companies that made ACE inhibitors and the Veterans' Administration (VA) where I was working. I didn't get any funding to run a "proper" study. So, one day in clinic in March 1994, I realized that I knew something that could save my patients, but I was waiting until I got money to prove it. I wasn't getting any money, and meanwhile my patients were still heading rapidly toward dialysis and then death in a couple of years.

I wound up treating my own two hundred kidney patients with higher doses of ACE inhibitors. Why higher doses? My argument was that kidney doctors had been using ACE inhibitors for ten years already and had gotten okay, but not great, results. We still couldn't stop kidney failure, especially for African Americans who have a ten times higher rate of kidney failure than Caucasians do. We had the right drug. I figured the only thing wrong had to be that we just weren't using a high enough dose.

So, I upped the dosage and I was right. The first patient I tried it on reversed his kidney failure. He got better and that wasn't supposed to happen. I was hooked. Another doctor left, leaving me with his 800 patients. I ran 1,000 patients on high-dose ACE inhibitors for the next three years and got fired from the VA for my positive results.

Why? The VA went "managed care" about two years after I started the program and mandated that all doctors had to prescribe exactly the same dosages. They weren't interested in my patient results even though they were 1,000 times better. At that point, I had been doing the same thing for two years already and morally I couldn't stop. They fired me in March 1998.

At that point, my lab had found that overactivity of ACE was behind 75 percent of human diseases. Now what to do? Getting fired from the VA in 1998 forced me into the private sector. I didn't want to move because my wife, who is also an MD, had a good job. I figured I would be more likely to get some money from the many angel investors than from the few federal sources who had already turned me down.

I used my own funds to support this first company. My mother had just died and left me $300,000. I used that to fund the lab for the first nine months and then I found some angels who were actually friends of mine from college and prep school. They brought in a third guy who they had known at Harvard Business School. He proceeded to destroy the company. He was telling me how to do the science, while not raising any money. They didn't want to do any disease management, they had no revenue plan, and it was clear that the guy who was putting most of the money in was only doing it so that his friend from business school could run the show. He had no interest in me controlling the company, although it was my company.

This first company eventually was sold. All the twenty thousand samples that I had collected were given to a private company and I have no access to them anymore. The loss of the money was bad; the loss of the samples was priceless.

Once it became clear that my first company was no longer under my scientific direction, I started another one. Why? I knew that my hunch was right. I knew where to look to find disease-causing genes. But it was my lack of control and the overall lack of financing that killed the first company.

I started a new company with the former scientific consultant and one of the former board members. This second company also soon failed because of disagreement over control. The two others didn't want it to be a disease management company. I did. I wanted to use a genotyping company we had visited in the Baltic. The other scientist didn't.

The way I found out that the second company failed was on a Monday morning. We had been negotiating a key license with a local university for over a month. We had a license agreement on our company letterhead. On Saturday, we had a telephone board meeting right after we got back from the Baltic. It ended with my usual plea for an operating agreement so we would know how to resolve disputes, such as which genotyping company we went with. On Monday morning, I found out that my two partners had started a new company without me. Furthermore, they had taken with them the negotiations for the key license we had been negotiating for a month with the local university, where the scientist partner was still employed. The university's tech transfer officer, who was good friends with the university scientist, didn't think twice about dropping the negotiations already underway with our company

If you believe in what you are doing, you have to continue.

and taking up negotiations with the scientist at his new company. I formally complained to the university. They said they would look into it and, of course, I'm still waiting three years later.

At this point, I had nothing. I had no money—the third partner was the "angel"—and I didn't have any financial backup. So I figured I would start writing patents. I wrote down everything I knew for a patent application. I started writing and I just kept going. As far as finding a backer, my plan was to just blanket all the biotech and pharmaceutical companies. I had given up on venture capitalists because I had pursued all of them with my private company. I figured I would just blanket all the companies that appeared in the throwaway journals and email everybody I could who had a biotech or pharmaceutical company. I figured that they needed results and that I knew where to find these disease genes.

I was fortunate that out of thousands of companies that I emailed, I got one that had just gotten funded by Research Capital. They were interested in doing additional deals so they put me in touch with Research Capital. Company number three was formed. Then September 11, 2001, happened and they cancelled the deal.

Back to the funding search. I couldn't find any in October 2001. Eventually, Research Capital funded the company with the provision that I find a businessperson who would be CEO. I again chose the wrong person. We got rid of him in September 2003, and promptly ran out of money. So, still believing that I was right, I operated the company by myself and didn't raise any money to speak of until January 2004. I didn't get paid from October 2002 until February 2004.

I kept going despite all of the trauma. I didn't have any options. I couldn't get an academic job any more. I had put up enough of a fuss at the VA and had appeared in a muckraking newspaper. Traditional physicians just don't do that sort of thing. My feeling was that these treatments were the difference between living and dying for my patients. I didn't feel like a federal agency should require me to kill my patients in order to keep my job. It seemed like a worthwhile fight to me. I learned a lot about the media and speaking out, all of which I'm using now.

There isn't a single thing that I learned that I haven't put to use. I would never have been able to operate completely solo if I hadn't essentially been put on house arrest by the VA for a year. You have to create your daily routine.

Basically, keeping going was being able to draw on prior tough experiences—realizing it wasn't the end of the world when they were occurring. It also helped that there was the lack of any alternative. It wasn't like I was being plied with offers to be head of this or that department.

Most important, I was absolutely convinced I was right. Not only was I convinced that I was right, but I also felt like I didn't have any moral alternative. I felt like I was pursuing the highest road possible. While I was fighting the VA, I got very religious.

I do think that the future is on my side. I have proven that I can prevent kidney failure. I know I can significantly delay emphysema and I can cure West Nile encephalitis. These are just three out of 150 diseases that I know that I can make an impact on.

I also feel that one thing that inspired me was just the knowledge that all I had to do was survive. George Washington only fought seven battles in seven years. He knew all he had to do was keep his army alive and he'd win. So, my goal was to just stay alive and eventually I'd win.

The light at the end of the tunnel now may still be a train headlight. We don't have enough financing yet. We just brought in about $1.5 million. We are going to need $100 million to do all the genotyping. It actually looks like an ongoing train engine rather than the end of the tunnel.

What I'm really passionate about is taking better care of patients and improving clinical outcomes. I found that you can do a lot better job when you know the disease-causing genes. We call ourselves a "Next Generation Disease Management" company because we use genomics to improve outcomes.

It hasn't been fun. However, what I am doing is important and I have to do this. I will continue until I die.

What I learned:

- If you believe in what you are doing, you have to continue.
- Failing companies do not mean failure. There is always another way to continue on, even if it is by yourself for a while. You will eventually find the right partners.

Applying the lessons learned to your business:

- Just because your company failed doesn't mean that you can't start another one with the knowledge that you gained. If you believe in what you are doing, then take what you learned and start again. Don't make those mistakes again.
- Make sure that you have agreements in place with your funding organization and partners delineating the duties of each, the milestones to be reached, and the penalties for not reaching those milestones. There should also be an agreement on the conditions that will trigger dissolving the partnership and how that dissolution will take place.

#50

EXPANSION BREEDS ISSUES
Lester Scaff
CEO, S&S Foods, Inc.

My father always told me that if I went into business for myself I could do better than working for someone else. So, I graduated from high school, got married, and in 1961, found my first store in Lake City, Florida.

I did have some experience because I had worked in my dad's store. I knew about handling customers and I knew about store work. My wife was with me 100 percent of the way.

She handled the cash register and the orders. I did the meats, produce, and swept the floor. We were doing okay, so I bought my second store.

I don't have a clue why I bought it except I had always wanted more. I had in mind multiple stores from the beginning. I had the opportunity to buy the second one and I did it. That was our biggest challenge because I had to learn how to manage people. It's fine when you run your own store and only one store. You are there. You handle the money and take it to the bank. You are handling everything else, too. You lock the store up at night and you open the store in the morning.

When you go into the second one, you can't be in two places at once. You have to have someone else to help you do it. Then your job turns into management and that is when you have to learn how to manage. So, that's what I did for a couple of years. I learned how to manage.

Of course, I was fortunate because I think there were more quality people at the time than there are today. I also had to learn perseverance. I had to learn to hang in there because there are all kinds of problems you have to confront, one after another and continuously.

Even today, forty-six stores later, there is always somebody chomping at you and somebody always wants your business. You've got to hang in. In retrospect, that is the most important thing: perseverance. That I learned.

You always have to fight the competition. Someone is always after your dollars and your business. You never get it to the point where you can relax and say, "Nobody is going to bother me now. I've got it made."

It isn't any fun when someone opens a store right next to you where one wasn't needed. You've got to fight. Neither one is going to make money in the beginning. You have to accept that fact. They usually open up with low prices, so you have to either match their price or go below them. It still turns out to be not profitable since a single storeowner does not have the overhead that you have.

We have the overhead, we have Worker's Comp, we have hospitalization, and we have a whole company of people who have benefits. They have none of these costs, so they can sell their stuff cheaper. But we still have to compete with them. It is a new competitor that we haven't dealt with in the past.

You have to handle each situation as it comes. We probably have a few stores out of forty-six that are really not profitable. But we are not going to close those stores because we are not going to give our competition the advantage. If they get away with it, they'll just open up more around us. We have to find a way to win not just against them, but we have to find a way to be profitable in those particular stores.

One of the other issues that we've confronted is a contamination issue. Several years ago, we didn't have any gasoline contamination laws or clean up laws. All of a sudden, the laws are enacted and they tell us that we have to have double wall pipes, etc. and we are forced to

All it takes in business is being willing to work and stay the course.

spend money to redo all of our gasoline installations. It is just another problem that we are presented with. I've learned that is just part of being in business.

I've been in business since 1961. I've had so many things happen, and I've seen lots of changes over the years, and I've had to adapt to them. And you know we don't like to adapt to change. When I first started off, it was just a store. We didn't even have fountain drinks. We sold bottled cokes and drinks. I hated it when all of a sudden the bigger competition out-of-town areas were starting to put in fountain drink machines. I said, "Holy cow! That will cost a lot of money." I didn't want to do that, but I had to make that change.

The other major change was gasoline. We didn't sell gasoline up until I had my seventh store. At the time, you had to service the cars. A customer couldn't pump his own gas. When I was forced to install gasoline, we put two pumps out front with lights over them. Eventually for us to survive, we had to do like everybody else. We had to get a big canopy and we changed into gas pumping instead of just being a convenience store.

I've always watched my competition. I go into the bigger convenience stores in the larger cities to see what they are doing. These are the things that I will probably be doing soon, so it's best to get prepared.

When things happen, you always get excited. It's hard when you can't see around the corner how you're going to make it work. However, I've been through enough "corners" over the years so that I know that we will eventually see how we will make it work. Perseverance will get us through.

What I learned:

- Even if you can't see around the corner, there is a vision there. The idea is you'd like to be able to see around the corner and have enough faith in yourself. Know that if you keep plugging along and persevere, then you will be able to get around that corner.

- We have a lot of people who can help. We teach our supervisors and other employees to treat the stores like they are their own stores, and to treat the money like it is their own money.
- My instruction to my employees is one commandment that Jesus gave: to love one another. I told the supervisors that they needed to love *all* the people who work for this company and do good for them by helping them make that bonus money. When you get to one of those years and can't give them that bonus, they won't think you love them very much. They are going to blame it on us.
- I've had a lot of success. I wasn't the smartest kid in school. However, I found that all it takes in business is to have determination and be willing to work and just stay the course.
- I can remember back in the beginning of the business I worked a lot of times because I enjoyed being in business for myself and that was the most important thing. That's what kept me going for a long time. In the beginning when you are paying all the bills, you don't really have any money and you go for years because all the money you get you put back in the business. One thing you don't do is spend your success before you get it.

Applying the lessons learned to your business:

- When you are going through a crisis, find others who have gone through it before and ask for advice. Ask what they would have done differently, the lessons they learned, and compare it to your situation. You'll find that you learned from that person and won't make those mistakes.

- Once you are successful, it's time to give back. You have an even bigger job to find a way to put that money where it is going to be good for mankind. Choose a way to give back that makes sense to you and contribute time and money. It will make you feel good and you will be surprised how it also helps your business.

PART TWO

WHAT YOU CAN DO ABOUT IT

CHAPTER THREE

CRITICAL SURVIVAL STRATEGIES

Fear begins when emotions take control and logic disappears.

The initial reaction to the nightmare, the gut-wrenching event for everyone I interviewed was emotional rather than logical. All went through the emotions of the situation, everyone reacting in their own personal way. Some cried, some screamed, some were quiet, some went to friends and people they trusted, some braved it alone...others went into deep prayer. Others did something people who've never experienced the fear or nightmare would laugh at: got into their cars, put the top down, and drove away screaming.

The overwhelming fact that emerged from the interviews is that everyone goes through it—challenges, hard times, problems, trauma, and nightmares. Call it what you'd like, everyone went through it.

Everyone reacted to it emotionally before they began the logic thought process.

At some point, logic begins to emerge. For some it was within minutes. For others it took days. Once logic took over, the decision-making process could begin. You ask yourself, "What are you going to do about it?" You begin dealing with the situation. You begin dealing with the fear. You deal with the unknown one step at a time.

If you are going through the fear and uncertainty, take comfort in the fact that you are not alone. Others have gone through it before you. Others will go through it after you. Here are some ways to help you get through it.

1. Pick Yourself Up, Dust Yourself Off, and Keep Going

All of the entrepreneurs faced terrible days. I never want to have another day like the day that I lost that sale, investment, and partner. However, I now know that if something similar happens, I can get through it.

Everyone I interviewed said the same thing. They now have the confidence that when bad things happen, they can face them, deal with them, and get through them. You never know how long the terrible things, the dark days, will last. However, you know that there is light at the end of the tunnel. You continue toward that light and eventually you will emerge.

In retrospect, everyone said they learned from the experience. Going through it was hell. However, that situation gave them the knowledge and the ability to handle other issues that arose later.

Lester Scaff really put it in perspective. Having been in business for over forty years and growing his business from one convenience store to forty-six stores, he had plenty of opportunities for fear and nightmares. His description, "I don't know what is around the corner," fits how he now thinks about and deals with challenges. Having more than forty years of experience has given him perspective, so he now can react quickly with confidence knowing that he can handle anything. He will persevere.

Another entrepreneur was very succinct. When he was in Vietnam, he was routinely shot at in combat. A customer was yelling at him because the entrepreneur didn't do something the customer thought should have been done. The entrepreneur's comment: "Yelling at me doesn't affect me. I've been shot at."

2. Learn to Deal with Your Emotions

When the nightmare hits, we react emotionally at first. Find a way to release the emotions quickly so that you can start thinking logically again.

If you're lucky, that emotion takes only a few minutes. When Christopher Pollock was in the hotel business and 9/11 hit, he had been through it before while he was running a hotel in the Virgin Islands and the United States invaded Iraq during the Kuwait war. Since he had been through it before, the emotional response was very short and he sprung into action, relying on his past experiences. Even though what happened during 9/11 turned out to be longer and much more devastating economically than the Virgin Islands situation, he was able to think clearly and get what had to be done, done.

Many of the men and one woman stated that they didn't get too stressed. Everyone said something like this: "I try to address the problem. What can I do immediately? What can I do tomorrow? Next week? Next month?" And they did what they could do every day to solve the problem.

Here are some physical things that may get you through the emotions:

Cry

Men and women cried when things happened. Tears, no matter how few, seem to be a good way to get rid of emotion for many entrepreneurs. Most of us don't like to be seen crying. When it hit me, I walked out the door of my office and went to the back of our office complex, sat down on the curb where no one could see me, and cried. Once the tears are gone, you usually feel better. The situation hasn't changed. However, the initial emotional hit is gone and you are in better shape to deal with the issues at hand.

Hugs

The physical touching of another human being helped some entrepreneurs. The person they hugged the most was their spouse. This is why spousal support is critical if you are married. In cases where the entrepreneur was single, most had a very close friend who would give them a hug when needed.

Scream

Get in your car, open the sunroof, and drive away screaming at the top of your lungs was the method used by Loretta Elbel to deal with the emotions of the situation. It worked for her.

Donna Fox explodes every once in a while. It gets rid of the stress for her. Usually it's at her husband who is there for support. He knows that she isn't exploding at him; just the situation.

Eat

There are two reactions here. Some entrepreneurs stop eating under stress. Others eat a lot. You may have "an Oreo moment." Food, specifically a bag of Oreos, was comfort to Jim Annis's wife when he told her he quit his job.

Throw Something

There is something satisfying about hearing the sound of breaking china against a wall. Each and every throw is emotional. You see the person or the thing in millions of tiny pieces. Then, you calm down as you pick up the broken dishes.

If you can't bear to buy some inexpensive dishes to throw, you can always throw a brick...a Styrofoam brick.

Our company has used these Styrofoam "anxiety bricks" to deal with frustrating telephone calls and other situations that cause stress. Throwing the anxiety brick at the wall doesn't hurt the wall, and always brings on laughter.

Laughter

Laughter is one of the best ways that I know of to decrease stress. For some reason, when you are laughing, you can't cry. The situation may be so absurd that you can't do anything other than laugh or cry. It's much better to laugh.

3. Find a Physical Way to Deal with the Ongoing Stress

Even though the emotion of the situation doesn't last long, getting through the dark days can take weeks, months, or even years. This can be extremely stressful on you. You have to find a way to decrease the effects of stress on you.

Exercise helps a lot of entrepreneurs. I started running at the age of forty-four and ran my first marathon three weeks before my forty-sixth birthday. I often say that I would be a basket case if I didn't run. For me, running gets rid of the stress. Bob Breaux ran every day when he walked away from the printing company. It helped him clear his mind and deal with the situation.

Many other entrepreneurs I spoke with also ran, cycled, or did some form of exercise. One took up karate and is going for her black belt. The exercise helped them deal with the inevitable hard times. Many times, it is during exercise that entrepreneurs got the ideas that helped them through the rough days. It helped decrease the effects of stress.

Tom Powell is a fitness instructor. It keeps him in shape and it forces him to exercise even if he "isn't in the mood" because he has to teach class.

One entrepreneur pulls weeds. She likes gardening and a handful of weeds per day helps get rid of the stress. Each weed is something that went wrong or somebody who did something. Pulling it out is like pulling out the problem.

Others had different hobbies that they enjoyed. When they did these hobbies, their mind wasn't on the business and they could relax doing something that pleased them. Often ideas came to them while they were enjoying their hobbies.

4. Believe in What You Are Doing

When I was doing the interviews and talked about what happened to me, one of the interviewees said that he would have quit. At the moment it happened, I didn't know what I was going to do. However, I was going on. I didn't quit because I believed in what I was doing.

Time after time entrepreneurs told me that the belief in what they were doing got them through the dark days. Every time something bad happened, they reminded themselves why they were doing what they were doing and continued on.

David Moscowitz continued through the demise of several businesses because he believes that what he is doing is important for the health of people. He worked alone for part of the time because he didn't have the funding to hire others to help him. Through the good days and the bad days, he continues on.

Tom Kemper has a similar story. He tells the story of his banker asking him why he is doing what he is doing. He explained that he is doing it for the health of the planet. He truly believes that someone must care for the future generations on earth. By doing his part, he is helping to save the planet for future generations.

Adria Manary never lost the belief in herself and her story despite the hardships that she went through trying to get her book published. At each obstacle, she reminded herself that it was important and she continued through.

Tim Hutchinson believed that his story and what happened to him was so important to share that he sold his truck to make it through.

Julia Barredo Willhite and her husband sold everything they owned, including their house and vehicles, to make sure employees got paid through the end of their final month in business. They made it through the bankruptcies and are back on their feet again.

If you truly believe that what you are doing is important, this belief alone can help you through the dark days.

5. Be Flexible

First, write the plan to resolve the situation. However, realize that the likelihood of following that plan to the letter is nil. You have to learn to be flexible. If a specific situation doesn't happen, you need to have a plan to go around it, go through it, or go in a totally opposite direction.

Eric Hansen is a master at this. When he bought the lawn care business he eventually sold, his business plan said, and he told his banker and others, that X, Y, and Z were going to happen. As it turned out, the exact opposite of X, Y, and Z actually happened. The business still was profitable and was sold. His banker remarked to him that the actual events were 180 degrees opposite of what the initial plan was. This was the first time that Eric realized this. However, Eric quickly recognized when something didn't work and tried something else.

Steve Saunders had to react when he got the letter stating that the customer wasn't going to pay the $750,000 they owed. He found flexible ways to raise cash. He refinanced as much as he could. As he puts it, "I didn't care about the interest rate. I only cared that I could get the cash."

6. Rely on People You Trust Outside the Business

Most of the time when someone asks us how business is, we say "great," even if sales are slow and we don't have a clue where next week's payroll is going to come from. As a rule, entrepreneurs don't trust anyone when discussing their business. And, even if we are doing great, we don't want anyone to know how great.

If your business is a partnership, you still need to find outsiders with whom you can discuss situations. The outsiders can provide perspectives that even the partners can't see because they are in the day-to-day running of the business with you.

Finding people you trust is critical. These are colleagues and true friends who you can rely on to listen and provide support and comfort as you are going through the dark days. For some entrepreneurs it was their spouse. Others told their spouse nothing about the business. One spouse remarked to her husband that she had to go out to dinner with him more often because the people they met in restaurants were his business associates and she learned what he was doing!

Find people you can be brutally honest with. These associates should also be brutally honest with you. They can provide a sounding board, advice, and encouragement as you are living the nightmare.

As one entrepreneur said, "At first, I talked to the wrong people and learned that I couldn't trust them. They stopped referring business to me. I soon found people I could trust who listened to me, believed in me and my abilities, and sent me back out with encouraging words."

Even though Barb Mather has not hired her first employee, she has a group of people she can celebrate with and a group that she can lean on in the tough times. Throughout her life, she has stayed with a core group of friends that she could lean on and rely on.

Pat Murphy would start another business if he could put together a strong team; both internal and external. He learned that you can't do it alone.

7. Have a Team Inside the Business

"Two heads are better than one" is an old cliché. However, many entrepreneurs found that they could trust their managers and employees. In fact, several, including Billie Redmond, Jeff Russell, Jim Annis, Lester Scaff, and many others, built their businesses around finding trustworthy employees.

Billie Redmond found that by talking with her employees (which she was initially reluctant to do), solutions to problems appeared from suggestions they made.

Pat Murphy also learned the hard way that he couldn't do everything. When the work wasn't up to his standards, rather than train and oversee, he chose to do the work himself, thus falling into what I call the "sell-produce curve." When you are selling, you can't produce and when you are producing, you don't have time to sell. So, you finish one job and don't have revenues until you sell the next job.

Kitty Ariza's partner vanished the first month she was in business. So, she tried to do it all herself too. Her goals were different from Pat Murphy's; she wanted to build credit in her name. When she accomplished this goal and had a profitable business, she was still alone. Her husband felt that she was spending too much time on it and she found another way to earn profits by inventing a product. She closed her profitable business and began another one that she could do by herself. It is very difficult to sustain a profitable, growing business without help.

Another entrepreneur learned to rely on her board. They helped her become a "real business" and she relies on their expertise.

Many of the partnerships are team arrangements. The best partnerships are where each partner brings a different strength to the business. All must contribute capital or credit. However, with different strengths, you have the best chance of success.

One company didn't have much of a chance without a CEO who joined the business. Then, to get funding, that

CEO had to bring in another partner who had raised venture capital before and built a successful business. Without these team players, the two inventors of the product would not have seen their product come to fruition.

Another manufacturer makes sure that she grows her employees' skills. She recognized long ago that she couldn't do it all herself. Her husband has complimentary skills to hers. She has grown and trained a management team to handle the growth of the business.

Most entrepreneurs find positive people they can rely on to suggest improvements, solutions to issues as they arise, and to weed out the bad employees.

8. Make a List

When you put things on paper, you often see the realities of what is happening. When Ron Detjen's banker told him to get all of his money out of his bank that day, he was reeling. Once the emotions settled down, he made a list of what needed to be done and when it would be done. That list helped him get through the tough times.

As the owner of the business where the bookkeeper stole money said, finding that someone stole money from your business is shocking. A list was necessary to find out exactly how much was stolen and what the true picture of accounts payable and accounts receivable were. Once these were done, then the action plan was put in place and the owner could handle the situation.

Lists help a lot. You can put your thoughts down on paper. You can often see that things aren't as bad as they appear in your imagination.

9. Write in a Journal

Writing down your emotions, your feelings, and what happened each day can help. You may never read the words again. However, other entrepreneurs have read what they wrote months or years before. When they read it a second or third time, they realize that a lot of the fear, uncertainty, and anxiety was just of the unknown. Once the issues became clear, they were prepared to handle them. And reading later puts perspective on what happened before. If you went through it once, you can do it again.

Many of the entrepreneurs who have been in business for decades rely on writing. They have reports of what happened in the past. These can be as simple as minutes from meetings that have occurred. They reread the reports when they need ideas to solve current challenges they are facing.

10. Go with Your Gut

Your instinct is usually right. If you truly listen to what it is saying, it is probably telling you the truth, even if you don't want to hear it. When I started the business, all of the people around me, except for a few, were fighting to get the business started on a much smaller scale. They were in fear for their jobs and wanted to continue spending until we ran out of money. Revenues are what count and my gut was telling me that. So, despite the objections of many people, we started the company.

Monica Y. Brown listened to her gut when her "backer" didn't pay her first invoices. She immediately stopped working for him and probably saved thousands of dollars.

Jeff Russell moved from Arkansas to Missouri on a gut feeling. He started his business in a new state where he knew no one. His gut said to do it and his business has been successful and profitable.

Larry Duckworth learned the hard way to listen to his instincts rather than his team. Had he done so and visited the client as soon as he saw a problem, he might not be part of an RFP and competing with giant companies for his survival right now.

Other entrepreneurs ignored their good sense when they wanted a particular outcome. One wanted to be the hero. Another let greed overtake his good sense.

If everyone around you is telling you something and you want to ignore it, find out why. Are emotions overriding your good sense?

11. Make the Tough Decisions

Sometimes when the situation occurs, you know that it is the end of doing business the way that you did it yesterday. You've got to make the tough decisions so that the business will survive. First, get through the emotion of the situation. When logic appears, then it is time to make the tough decisions.

Victoria Kamm laid off 150 people the day after the government announced that it did not have the funding to enforce the refrigerant monitoring regulations. She knew business was over as they had done it before. It was a tough, painful, but necessary decision for the survival of the business.

Loretta Elbel had to decide which of the customers came first, second, etc. She had to decide who got product first. She risked cancelled orders and angry customers. However, she was open with all of them and gave them realistic shipping dates.

Christopher Pollock knew what he had to do. It was going to be difficult. However, he met with his management teams and immediately got started making the tough decisions.

Tough decisions are not easy decisions. However, they are critical for the survival of your business.

12. Find a Spiritual Way to Deal with the Terror

Almost all entrepreneurs I interviewed talked about having a deep faith. They prayed a lot or meditated a lot when the tough times hit. The type of religion didn't matter. The geographic location of the entrepreneur didn't matter.

David Moscowitz became deeply religious during one of his tougher times. It gave him the strength to keep going.

Rochele Hirsch found a seminar leader to help her through the blockage. She learned why she kept sabotaging her efforts. Once she got through the issues, her business began to flourish.

Rich Schmidt is a pastor. He got "tapped on the shoulder" by God to start the new church. He kept this message and his faith while putting down roots in a new community, even when he didn't know whether the church would be successful.

Lamar Lawrence said the challenges he went through were a great test of his faith and probably made him stronger. He found out a lot about himself and strengthened his faith in God.

And what about Siney Jordan? She absolutely states that it was her faith in God that got her through. She wanted to quit at times. Her husband wanted to quit. They prayed and asked God why He was putting them through this if He wanted them to have the building. They got the message to keep going. They did and ultimately prevailed.

Others turned to ministers, daily prayers, or meditations to get them through. Even now that some of the entrepreneurs are through the dark days, they still meditate and pray.

Everyone was searching for answers to help him or her through their crises. Most mentioned turning to a higher power to help guide them through the dark days.

13. An Angel Might Appear

When one entrepreneur was six weeks away from shutting the doors, an angel appeared in the form of an investor. This investor took an interest in what the company was doing and invested $500,000. It saved the company. The angel went on to become CEO and facilitate another round of funding for the technology start-up.

Bob Breaux's angel appeared in a different form. When he started his second business, his CPA invested with him by supplying the credit so he could get a loan. When Bob invested more in the business, he wanted to alter the percentage that each partner got in the business. The CPA agreed and reduced his share to 20 percent. When it was time to distribute the shares, the CPA told Bob to put the shares into two stock certificates each with a 10 percent share. When Bob handed him the shares, he turned them over and assigned them to each of Bob's two children.

Gary Markle's angel was the government. By mandating that the banks have the type of software his company was producing, the government saved Gary's business.

Tom Kemper's is a person who lets him use their condominium in the hill country free of charge when he needs a respite.

You never know when a chance meeting or telephone conversation will produce the idea you need to get through the darkness.

14. Surround Yourself with Positivity

Over and over again, entrepreneurs told me that they tried to find positive people and things in their lives. Many listened to motivational and uplifting tapes every day. "There is so much negativity in the world that you have to listen to something positive every day." Tom Hopkins (author of *How to Master the Art of Selling*) and Jim Rohn, an internationally known business philosopher, were mentioned more than once.

One had a coach who made a CD for him every two weeks. He listens to this in his car and it keeps him on track.

You can get dragged down if all you listen to and hear are negative ideas, negative happenings in the world, and negative people. Pauline Cormier learned early to talk with positive people who would encourage her in her business.

Christine Kloser had the yin and yang in her life until she got New Entrepreneurs, Inc., up and going. The negative was everything that was happening with the yoga studio. The positive was the new group she was creating to help women in creative, positive ways.

Her comment is, "Surround yourself with people who have a 'you can' attitude rather than a 'you can't' attitude. It's your responsibility to seek out and find like-minded people who are going to lift you up and make you believe more in yourself than you might in the beginning. The majority of the population lives in 'I can't,' fear, doubt, and worry. You shouldn't be around these types of people."

15. Have Patience

Give yourself time. As entrepreneurs, we want the bad times over immediately. Patience is not usually one of our strong points. However, time does put perspective on the situation. You can review what happened, what you learned, and how you will deal with a similar situation next time.

The need for time and patience doesn't mean a lot when you are going through the nightmare, the fear, and the uncertainty. It doesn't help when someone you trusted betrayed you. The key is to learn from the event.

In the future, it won't seem as bad because you are dealing with the situation logically rather than emotionally. You won't forget because as one entrepreneur said, "Even though it is ten years later, I still get mad when I think about the situation. Then logic takes over and I know that 'what goes around, comes around,' and they will experience their own tough times at some point."

When my husband read my story, his comment to me was "I expected more invective in it." If it had been a year earlier, there might have been. Time gives us perspective. You learn from the situation and move on.

All entrepreneurs go through challenges and nightmares. You go through fear of the unknown. Eventually the unknown becomes known. Then the dark days turn into light. Sometimes the darkness lasts for minutes, other times for years. Have faith that you will get to - the light.

CHAPTER FOUR

REALITIES OF PARTNERS

A partnership is a business marriage. Make sure that you know whom you are getting into bed with.

If you have partners, you need to know how they react under pressure before it begins. How will they handle the inevitable times when cash is tight? How will they react when you are thirty days from running out of money?

Gary Markle talks about absolutely knowing the personality styles of the people you start a business with. Just because you worked with those people at larger companies does not mean that you will be compatible in a smaller company. In a subsequent business that failed, one of the reasons that it failed was that the partners were incompatible. Now Gary mentors and teaches others to really know and understand whom you are getting into business with.

You need to know what you are getting into before you sign on the dotted line. Someone may react totally differently than you've ever seen before when under stress of not getting a paycheck.

If you don't know the person, check him or her out thoroughly before starting, even if a friend introduced you. Check out that person's social security number. If he is a sales person, ask to see his W-2 for the past few years. Great salespeople usually don't mind bragging about their sales abilities.

You have to discuss the what-ifs. Ron Detjen talks about the business plan that you've put together. If the goal is selling ten widgets each month to have a profitable month, what happens if you only sell nine widgets and the promise of the tenth? You're not profitable. What happens if this continues for several months? When do you quit? When do you walk away? The answers to these questions must be discussed before the partnerships begin.

If you are putting money into the business, your partners have to put money in too. Everyone who is a partner needs to have a financial commitment of some kind. If the partner doesn't have cash, then putting up collateral is an acceptable alternative. I learned this lesson the hard way. If your partner is not willing to sign on the dotted line for bank loans or investor loans, he is not your partner, no matter what he says. That person will make different decisions because there is no risk on his part. And those decisions often are not in the best interest of the company. They are in his best interest. That person will be more willing to hire people because his money is not on the line. You will be at odds with your partner when the money gets tight and payroll/loans need to get paid.

What happens if more money needs to be invested in the business? Lamar Alexander learned this lesson from a savvy partner. When they didn't have enough money to pay the rent during the off season because they had started another business that was losing money, his partner very succinctly said that he wasn't pouring gasoline on a fire. He wasn't going to throw good money away. They had to resolve the situation with the cash that they had. And they found a way to do it. His partner, realizing that even though he could put more money in the business, wasn't going to do it until they found a way to be profitable.

On the other hand, Frank Schimicci's partners poured money on the fire when the business continued to lose money. They still thought they could turn it around, believed in Frank, and wrote a check.

How will your spouse handle the rough times?

If the people you are working with are married, you need to know whether their spouses will support the business in good times and during the rough times. It doesn't matter whether the business is in a start-up phase or has been in business for many years. You need support at home. There is enough stress in a business environment without having to go home to additional stress. If a partner's spouse wants a steady paycheck, then what will happen when the paycheck doesn't appear one week or for several weeks? How much additional stress will be brought on the partnership? Will the partner quit because the spouse is lobbying for a steady paycheck?

Even without partners, if you are married, you need to know how your spouse will handle the bad times.

You also need to know whether you have the support of your spouse when tough times hit. Many times, you don't know until it happens. Tom Kemper's ex-wife couldn't handle "living on the edge" anymore. She didn't talk with him about it. One day he came home and the house was empty. She was gone.

Another entrepreneur believes in what he is doing even more than his marriage. He has sacrificed his marriage for the business. This was his choice and he understands fully the consequences of his actions. In his mind, his contributions to society through his business are more important than his marriage.

A third entrepreneur, who had been in business with his wife, realized after ten years that they couldn't work together. So, they split up as business partners. She is running the business and he has started another one. They are still happily married.

One of the entrepreneurs in this book had the support of her husband through two of the three major crises.

Now the support is lukewarm. He felt that she has spent enough money. They have to save for the children's education and he feels that she shouldn't be spending her money on the business anymore. She longs for the continued support, but doesn't get the same conviction and help from her husband anymore.

When the nightmare hit me, my husband was extremely supportive and strong. He encouraged me to keep going. In fact, his discussions for weeks centered on getting the business operating until he sounded like a broken record. At that point, he had more confidence in me than I had. I was lucky to have someone to rely on who believed in me and who was stronger at that point than I was.

Others found similar situations to mine. They could lean on their spouse when the challenge hit. One couple working in the business together has a ritual of walking every night. It was extremely helpful when the bottom dropped out of the market and one of their major customers didn't order product for eighteen months. Their nightly walks provided the communication avenue to discuss feelings and fears, and generate ideas on how to handle the situation.

Donna Fox's husband is her sounding board. She has a tendency to keep things inside until they erupt. Then she explodes, usually to her husband. He understands that the explosion is not directed at him. It's her way of getting the stress out. And she does it with someone she trusts.

If your spouse is supportive, you have a much easier time getting through the uncertain times. There is encouragement through the dark days rather than additional stress.

Make sure you know who your partners are and the answers to what-if questions before you start a business together. Even though you may not physically go to bed with them each night, you are usually spending more time with them than with your real bed partner.

CHAPTER FIVE

THE 7 GREATEST MYTHS OF BUSINESS OPERATIONS

As a result of the research and stories that our entrepreneurs graciously shared with me, I've distilled seven myths of operating a business that can quickly get you in trouble. Avoiding these myths won't keep you out of trouble. However, you can be the third type of businessperson and learn from the mistakes of others.

Myth #1: The product is so good it sells itself.

One of the mistakes made was to spend a lot of time on design of the product, the store location, and the services to be offered to customers. You open your doors and announce to the world "I'm here, come get me." You wait and get few sales. Or, you overestimate the space you need and overhead kills you.

You can have a great product, great production, and great cash reserves. If you don't have great sales and marketing, the other "greats" don't matter. *No* product sells itself.

You have to constantly promote. Everyone sells, from the person answering the telephone to you as the head of the company. If you—the owner, the CEO, the president—thinks, "I'm not a sales person," you're kidding yourself. You have the most important sales job. You have to convince customers why they should buy from you as well as sell your employees on the company so they will believe in and sell your company's products.

The best person at selling your products and services is you, the entrepreneur. Julia Barredo Willhite says that she shouldn't have hired an agency since she knew how to do it from experience. She feels that she is best at selling her products and services.

You'll often be called in to close a difficult sale. Most people are impressed that the business owner is taking his or her time to be interested in the sale and the customer. The higher you go and the larger your company, the more critical the entrepreneur's sales skills. You can often make one telephone call to a president of the prospective customer's company or meet him at a trade association, or another venue outside the office, to agree to a deal. The details are left to lower ranking individuals. The message from the top is "do the deal."

No product sells itself. Constant attention and nurturing of customers and prospective customers is critical for success.

Myth #2: Start your own business to get rich fast.

Some of the entrepreneurs whose stories appear in this book were thrown into business from good paying jobs. They expected the same level of success and income from the outset of their business. They were rudely awakened. Some didn't adjust their standard of living and eventually filed bankruptcy before they learned to live on less income.

Others had spouses who expected the same level of income when the businesses were started. This *never* happened. As a result, there were strained relationships in marriages. The entrepreneurs never gave up the belief that they were right, even when cash was extremely scarce. Their belief in themselves and the fact that they were right kept them going...sometimes to the detriment of the marriages.

None started their businesses with the intention of getting rich. All had something to prove, either to themselves or others. Some had a mission and wanted to do something important, as David Moscowitz and Tom Kemper did. In fact, they would have been richer had they stayed in the "corporate world." In most entrepreneurs' personalities, restlessness won't let them stay in the corporate world. They either leave or are kicked out because they no longer "fit in."

Some of the entrepreneurs, like Billie Redmond, knew that they were pioneers. They knew that it would take long, hard hours to achieve what they wanted to achieve. Some have hit it big; some have decided to stay small. All knew that by starting their own businesses, they were going to get rich slowly, if at all.

Myth #3: The perfect partnership: I have the concept and the bank has the money.

Bankers want to loan you money when you don't need it. Steve Saunders' bank had said on multiple occasions that they would increase the line of credit...right up to the day that Steve needed it.

There are places that you can go for loans to start your business. These are usually referred to as friends, family, and fools. Unless you have a lot of collateral, bankers aren't willing to risk a loan.

In addition, venture capitalists and others who lend money (other than friends and family) want to see customers. They want to see that you have revenues and that your idea is not just an idea but also a living, breathing product or service that people will pay money for.

One entrepreneur learned this. He helped two software engineers who started in their garage build a business. The investors held all the cards. Initially it was a nice product with no customers. It was supposed to work; but did it? The investors were taking a chance on unproven technology. They had the money that the engineers needed to continue. From the engineers' position, they were between a "rock and a hard place" and had no other choice but to accept the terms of the venture capitalists if they wanted to keep the company and their dream alive.

Concepts don't count in the real world. Customers do.

Myth #4: I'll give the customer a discount and make it up on the next sale.

Many times, we think that we can entice a customer to purchase our products by giving discounts and then get full price the next time the customer buys. Unfortunately, the next time the customer buys, he is expecting to pay the same price as he did before. He thinks that the discounted price is the normal price and you're stuck with the discounts. It is unlikely that you will ever make up the difference on the next sale.

If you want several levels of prices, then you have to set up those tiers before you begin promoting your products and services. If you want to give a discount, make sure there is a reason for the discount. The customer should be giving you something in return.

Pat Murphy sold service agreements in his heating and air-conditioning company. If a customer was willing to sign a piece of paper agreeing to a heating and a cooling check on his furnace and air-conditioning system each year, Pat gave that customer a discount on all service work.

You might also give discounts for volume. Karen Price routinely uses discounts for volume because she can buy at better prices when the customer orders a greater number of checks, business cards, or other printed materials.

One entrepreneur learned the hard way that you can't give it away. If someone said that they wanted her services and couldn't afford them, she often gave away the seminars and meetings hoping the customer would pay the next time. They customer didn't come back. She learned that something free has no value to the customer.

Know why you are giving a discount. Give it for a specific reason. You won't make it up on the next sale.

Myth #5: If my competition can sell for that price, so can I.

Maybe. You've got to know your costs. Your competition may have determined a more cost-efficient way to sell what you are selling. She may have cheaper labor, a better supplier with better prices, or lower selling costs. If you automatically drop your price to meet the competition, you may quickly find yourself in a cash crunch and out of business.

Overhead can also kill your company. One anonymous entrepreneur looked at the competition that had larger stores and thought that his company had to increase the size of their stores to meet the competition. What they found was that the additional overhead was too costly and the larger stores caused larger cash flow problems.

Don't look at what your competition is doing with respect to pricing. If your price is higher, find the value to the customer in your higher price. Sell that value to the customer.

This is what Larry Duckworth does all of the time. He finds hidden value in the companies he runs. His current learning-based software company competes head-on with other similar services. It uses some of the same educational programs that others can also sell. However, it's the extras that his company provides to its customers that make the valuable difference. The extraordinary way they take care of the customer and the customer's needs are critical to his company's success.

Always look at the competition to see what they are doing. Larry Scaff does this constantly. He goes into his competitors' stores to keep abreast of trends, current prices, and what products he will be providing.

However, before you change prices or give discounts, find out how the competition can do that. Look at your costs and determine whether you should drop your price or add more value. An automatic assumption that you can meet your competition's price is an assumption that may get you out of business.

Myth #6: My employees are my friends.

Your employees are not your friends. Your employees are being paid to do a specific task. Your partners are not your friends. If you get into business with friends, many times the friendships are gone because you don't know how your friends will react under different stressful situations.

Gary Markle talks about this constantly. One of his businesses, which he started with friends, failed because the friends reacted very differently when cash flow was tight.

You have to balance friends with "friendly," because in today's workplace, people are looking for a place to have personal relationships. That's what makes drawing the line between friends and "friendly" so difficult.

If you do things socially, you need to do things socially with everybody. Don't single out an employee for meals. If you have lunch or dinner with one person in your department, then you have to have lunch or dinner with everyone. This shows that you are being fair and not playing favorites.

Discipline with fairness. You can't let one person get away with doing something and the others not get away with it. If you are doing this with a perceived friend, then this will demoralize other employees. Everyone has to play by the same rules. And if someone isn't following the rules, the same discipline must adhere to all.

If an employee comes to you with marital problems, financial problems, or other personal problems, these should never be discussed with anyone else. However, you need to know what is going on and how it may affect his or her job performance. Despite these problems, the employee still has a job...and must be reminded of this.

So, be friendly with the employees, just don't be friends. You have to interact socially. Just monitor your interactions and make sure that you aren't playing favorites.

Myth #7: I will have more free time and I won't have to answer to anybody.

All of the entrepreneurs interviewed for this book routinely put in more hours than they did working for another company that wasn't theirs. You have more freedom to schedule your time. If you have to leave during the day, normally you can do it. However, you'll often find yourself working longer that day to make up for the time that you missed during the day.

You won't have to answer to anybody; you just have to answer to everybody—your employees, your customers, your banker, your insurance agent, and everyone else who wants to sell you something or you want to sell something to. Everyone wants a piece of your time.

Yes, you make the final decision. If you want to grow the business, then you have to learn to delegate some of those decisions and follow up. If you want to remain small and in control, then you don't have to delegate. Smaller businesses are totally dependent on your efforts. If something happens to you the likelihood is that the business will not survive. You have to make the right choice for your business and you.

The toughest thing for some of the entrepreneurs to do was to let go. Several tried and found that their employees "didn't do it like they did" and "didn't do it up to their standards." So, they went and did it themselves. Some, like Loretta Elbel, quit because they didn't want to work that hard anymore. Others shrunk their businesses so that they could have control and a family life.

If you believe in what you are doing so strongly that it is more important than family, then you spend more time on what you are doing and suffer the consequences of divorce and children with emotional problems. Several of the entrepreneurs in this book have experienced this.

One of the questions I was asked when I was applying for a membership in a business group was how many hours I worked. I told them zero because I don't consider what I do work. I love what I do and enjoy coming to the office as did most of the entrepreneurs...even in the tough times.

We also find a way to make it work with our families. Many, including myself, have raised our children in our offices. My daughter knew the UPS man, the FedEx man, and the postal deliveryman before she really knew what a kid was. She started coming to the office when she was two weeks old. As a ten-year-old, she remarked to me when my partner left for a "safe" job, "Doesn't he know that there is nothing risk free in this world?" It surprised me at the time. However, I realized that she was learning more about life than any school could teach her.

Children of the entrepreneurs interviewed either become great business owners, marry business owners, or want nothing to do with a business of their own. Several, such as one manufacturer's daughter, have children who have gone on to create great businesses of their own. Others have married entrepreneurs and know what to expect. They may not be involved with the business themselves, but provide a great deal of support and understanding. Others have children who want nothing to do with business because they've watched their parents suffer and work too hard (from their perspectives).

You don't have more free time as an entrepreneur. You do have more ability to schedule your time. For most of the owners interviewed, their time was spent on something that they love and believe in. They are willing to put in longer, harder hours to accomplish what they want to accomplish. This love and belief helps them keep the faith and helps them work through the dark days and into the light.

CHAPTER SIX

WORDS OF WISDOM

The entrepreneurs profiled in this book gave many words of wisdom to current and future entrepreneurs. They gave them from the heart in hopes that their words will help other entrepreneurs with their businesses.

- Your belief in yourself—why you are doing what you are doing—will get you through.

- You can get what you want if you persevere.

- Murphy's Law rules. Plan for the unexpected because that is what is going to happen. If you don't get upset by that and just keep right on going, you will work through the problems. You will prevail. Just don't think it is going to be an easy, magic thing.

- React to situations as they unfold, even if it is difficult.

- During crisis times, ask yourself, "What can I do today?" And do it. Usually, you can't solve the whole problem at once. Bite off a piece each day.

- Listen to your gut.

- You have to have a plan from start to finish. It doesn't mean that it will happen exactly that way, but you won't go zigzagging either. A plan is like a living, breathing document. Though it should change as situations dictate, it should also keep you pointed straight at your goals.

- Don't get stressed. Address the problem. Look at the logic of the situation and get done what needs to get done.

- Always think of how you can improve the company, make it better, and cut costs.

- When things are going well, try not to think that things are going well. If you do, you may start doing stupid things like making expensive development expenditures or trying to do something you know nothing about.

- Don't ask employees to do what you are not prepared to do yourself.

- The world is not black and white. It is shades of gray. You make that adjustment as you grow and mature. Going through these processes and moving from a black and white world to a gray world does cause a little fear. Once you realize that, you learn to adjust your thinking and your expectations. You need to have very realistic expectations. You will be forced by the venture capitalist world to do this and that can be difficult. You still hold your optimism, but the reality of control, how much control you have, how much control you have in the future, the control of the company and its direction, how rich you may be some day, etc., gets readjusted very quickly.

- Watch your competition. You need to react to what they are doing.

- If you see a profit in the first year or two, it is a gift.

- Pioneer work is tough. If you believe in your products and they are needed, you have to sell their benefits and convince the market of their benefits. The missionary work can't last long if you want to eat.

- You are very fortunate to do something that you really love. Many people hate their jobs. In that one respect, you are very lucky.

- God will come through if you have faith and trust in God. If you are doing what God wants, then things will work. There is nothing like going through an experience that can prove that to you.

- Just because you failed at something doesn't mean that you are a failure as a human being. Now you can go in a better direction and use it as a learning experience. The failure can be a blessing.

- Your behavior and attitude surely drive how the business does from a day-to-day emotional basis. If you walk into your business and your positive mental attitude is not there, it really can hurt.

- The "deal of a lifetime" comes around every couple of months.

- The most important asset of any company is your employees. You need the right employees in the right jobs.

- If you want to lead people on a difficult journey, and you're willing to be brutally honest about the risks and rewards, nearly anyone will follow you.

- Never let one customer represent more than 25 percent of your business.

- Keep your sense of humor.

- The people who win are the people who get through the tough times, put it behind them, and still go on.

- When it's your business you can't abdicate overall responsibility. You can't abdicate the checkbook.

- You can get through the tough times with a great product and sales ability. You have to sell a problem solution. You have to show your customers that you can save them time and money.

- Good news isn't usually as good as it sounds and bad news isn't usually as bad as it sounds.

- Do something that has an impact that you feel passionate about. Build something.

- Surround yourself with people who have a "you can" attitude rather than a "you can't" attitude. It's your responsibility to seek out and find like-minded people who are going to lift you up and make you believe more in yourself than you might in the beginning. The majority of the population lives in

"I can't" fear, doubt, and worry. You shouldn't be around these types of people.

- You have to be focused to be successful. Good things will happen. Bad things will happen. Keep the focus and remember why you are doing what you are doing.

- When you are successful, it is your responsibility to give back. Redistribute the wealth for the good of mankind.

ACKNOWLEDGMENTS

A very special thank you goes to each of the entrepreneurs who shared their stories with me. All were heartfelt, truthful, and sometimes painful to recall. I appreciate your candor and willingness to help others who will follow in your footsteps. For those of you who haven't emerged into the light, I hope you will get there soon.

Writing and publishing a book is a partnership. To Peter Lynch, Jill Amack, and countless others behind the scenes at Sourcebooks, thank you for making this partnership a very pleasant experience.

Next, I would like to thank Brenda Bethea, my assistant for more than fourteen years. She has watched the growth, the failures, the near misses, and the successes over the years. Until the writing of this book, she hadn't transcribed dictation for a long time. I appreciate her nimble fingers, dedication, no-nonsense style, and support in this and other endeavors.

I would be remiss if I didn't thank my parents for their love and support over the years. My father taught me that when bad things happen, pick yourself up, dust yourself off, and keep going. I did it, Daddy, despite how hard it was at times. And to my mother, who was there to lend an ear and give me a hug whenever I needed it. You both always supported my various endeavors even when you thought I was nuts. Thank you.

To my sixteen-year-old daughter, Kate, who lived through the years of tough times as we were building the various businesses. I know that it was definitely hard being a kid, getting sick of hearing your parents talking about business all the time, watching the lack of money, feeling your parents' stress, and hearing your parents say "no" when we didn't have the money to do something all of your friends were doing. You got an education about the real world that you'll never get in school. I hope you use the knowledge successfully in your future endeavors as an adult.

Last, but not least, to my husband, Bob. Even though I don't always say it and I don't always show it, a million thank you's are not enough. The journey we're traveling together hasn't always been fun. But it's never been dull. Without you, I wouldn't have gotten through the tough times. At times, you believed in me more than I believed in myself. So, this time I'm saying it in print, thank you.

INDEX

A

associations, 22, 31, 58

B

bank, 27, 58, 110
    relationship, 28
belief, 253, 254, 255, 285
business, 4, 15, 19
    bankruptcy, 15, 149, 151, 214
    communication, 41, 42, 109, 128, 192, 196, 222
    creativity, 15, 21, 124, 222
    failure, 4, 8, 35, 36, 69, 141, 236, 288
    family, 70, 109
    goals, 54, 58, 146, 227

N
networking, 31

P
partners, 10, 25, 110-113, 201, 236, 267-269
patience, 266

R
records, keeping, 179

S
sales, 23, 77, 217
seven myths, 273
    bank, 276, 277
    competition, 278, 279
    discounts, 277, 278
    employees, 279-281
    product, 273-275
    rich, 275, 276
    time, 281-283
Small Business Administration (SBA) loan, 101, 112, 147
stress, 26, 32, 35, 40, 85, 86, 87, 101, 162, 163, 213, 252, 253, 270, 286

V
venture capital, 52-54, 101, 276

ABOUT THE AUTHOR

Ruth King is a serial entrepreneur. Over the past twenty-five years, she has owned seven businesses. Her first business, Business Ventures Corporation, began operations in 1981. Through Business Ventures Corporation, she travels throughout the United States coaching, training, and helping small businesses achieve their business goals.

She is especially proud of one contractor she helped climb out of a big hole. He started with a negative $400,000 net worth fifteen years ago and is still in business today...profitably and with a positive net worth.

After twelve years on the road, doing two hundred flights per year, she knew there had to be a better way to reach contractors and other small businesspeople who wanted to build their businesses and train their employees. Her husband came up with the technology. As a result, ProNetworkTV, Inc., and its first channel, HVACChannel.tv, were born. The next channel, BusinessTVChannel.com, was built on the success of the first. This is television on the Internet. Information when you want it...where you want it...for less than the cost of lunch.

ProNetworkTV, Inc., is one of three companies that Ruth currently is an owner/partner in. She has been involved with many different businesses over the years with a wide range of interests, including music, videographic production, healthy house products, and T-shirts.

Ruth is passionate about helping adults learn to read, photography, and marathon races (she ran the Boston Marathon in April 2004 and 2005). She helped start an adult literacy organization in 1986 that currently serves over one thousand adults per year.

Ruth holds bachelor's and master's degrees in chemical engineering from Tufts University and University of Pennsylvania, respectively. She also holds an MBA in finance from Georgia State University.

She has written many manuals for contractors, including the popular Keeping Score series: *Financial Management for Contractors, Improving Profitability and Productivity,* and 21 *Ways to Keep Your Honest Employees Honest. The Ugly Truth about Small Business: 50 Things that Can Go Wrong and What You Can Do about It* is her latest book.

Ruth has spoken for national and state associations' meetings, national and local trade shows, manufacturers, distributors, and others in forty-nine of fifty states. She is a down-to-earth, thought-provoking speaker who will provide audiences with ideas that will inspire them and help them earn more profits. She is available for radio and TV interviews, in-store book signings, discussions, lectures, and seminars, and she is available worldwide, depending on her schedule.